# America's Haunted
## UNIVERSITIES

# About the Author

Matt Swayne is a journalist and writer, currently working as a research writer at Penn State. He's spent more than a decade reporting for community newspapers in the central Pennsylvania area and has freelanced for major newspapers and publications. More recently, he has worked on a book project with Eilfie Music on her adventures as a paranormal researcher for the show *Paranormal State*. Born on Halloween, he has always had an interest in folklore and the paranormal. That interest and his connection to Big Ten universities stirred this book project.

# To Write to the Author

If you wish to contact the author or would like more information about this book, please write to the author in care of Llewellyn Worldwide, and we will forward your request. Both the author and the publisher appreciate hearing from you and learning of your enjoyment of this book and how it has helped you. Llewellyn Worldwide cannot guarantee that every letter written to the author can be answered, but all will be forwarded. Please write to:

Matt Swayne
⁄ Llewellyn Worldwide
2143 Wooddale Drive
Woodbury, MN 55125-2989

Please enclose a self-addressed stamped envelope for reply,
or $1.00 to cover costs. If outside the USA, enclose
an international postal reply coupon.

Many of Llewellyn's authors have websites with additional information and resources. For more information, please visit our website at: www.llewellyn.com.

# America's Haunted

# UNIVERSITIES

## Ghosts That Roam Hallowed Halls

### MATTHEW L. SWAYNE

Llewellyn Publications
Woodbury, Minnesota

First Edition
First Printing, 2012

Book design by Bob Gaul
Cover art: Tower: iStockphoto.com/Duncan Walker
        Ravens: iStockphoto.com/Igor Djurovic
Cover design by Kevin R. Brown
Editing by Edward Day

Llewellyn Publications is a registered trademark of Llewellyn Worldwide Ltd.

**Library of Congress Cataloging-in-Publication Data**
Swayne, M. L.
  America's haunted universities: ghosts that roam hallowed halls/Matthew L. Swayne.—1st ed.
      p. cm.
  Includes bibliographical references (p. 215).
  ISBN 978-0-7387-3080-6
1. Haunted universities and colleges—United States.  2. Ghosts—United States.  I. Title.
  BF1478.S93 2012
  133.1'22—dc23
                    2012020554

Llewellyn Publications
A Division of Llewellyn Worldwide Ltd.
2143 Wooddale Drive
Woodbury, MN 55125-2989
www.llewellyn.com

Printed in the United States of America

# Contents

*Introduction: A Lesson in the Paranormal: 1*

**1  Student Union Buildings and Student Centers: 5**

Indiana Memorial Union—Indiana University: 6

La Casa, Latino Cultural Center—
  Indiana University: 10

O'Connell House—Boston College: 11

Willard Straight Hall—Cornell University: 13

Healy Hall—University of Georgetown: 14

The Dining Hall and Other Fighting Irish Ghosts—
  University of Notre Dame: 16

**2  Dormitories and Residence Halls: 19**

Rooming with the Paranormal: 19

Strong Hall—University of Tennessee: 20

Read Hall Dormitory—Indiana University: 22

Currier Hall—University of Iowa: 23

Slater Hall—University of Iowa: 25

Pioneer Hall—University of Minnesota: 26

Sanford Hall—University of Minnesota: 27

Watts Hall—Penn State: 28

Runkle Hall—Penn State: 30

Syme Residence Hall, Bragaw Residence Hall—
  North Carolina State: 32

Thayer Hall—Harvard University: 33

Weld Hall—Harvard University: 35

Haunted Houses—Harvard University: 36

Massachusetts Hall—Harvard University: 38

Ecology House—Cornell University: 40

Risley Hall—Cornell University: 41

Maricopa Residence Hall—University of Arizona: 42

Freeman Hall—Iowa State University: 43

Barton Hall—Iowa State University: 45

Linden Hall—Iowa State University: 46

Perkins Hall—Ohio University: 47

More Ohio University Haunts: 49

Bruce Hall—University of Pittsburgh: 50

Halcyon House—Georgetown University: 54

Room 4714—West Point: 57

Thayer House—West Point: 59

## 3  Classrooms and Administrative Buildings: 63

English Building—University of Illinois: 65

Lincoln Building—University of Illinois: 67

Psychology Building—University of Illinois: 68

Old Bryce or Kilgore House—
  University of Alabama: 69

Smith Hall—University of Alabama: 72

Tyson Hall—University of Tennessee: 74

Career Development Center—Indiana University: 76

Old Botany Building—Penn State: 77

Science Hall—University of Wisconsin: 78

Morrill Hall—University of Maryland: 80

Marie Mount Hall—University of Maryland: 81

H. J. Patterson Hall—University of Maryland: 82

Winslow Hall—North Carolina State: 83

1911 Building—North Carolina State: 84

Spring Hill House—North Carolina State: 85

Old Main—University of Arizona: 86

The Farm House—Iowa State University: 87

The Cathedral of Learning—
  University of Pittsburgh: 90

Alumni Hall—University of Pittsburgh: 100

Crosley Tower—University of Cincinnati: 102

The Ridges—Ohio University: 104

Wilson Hall—Ohio University: 105

The Main Building—University of Notre Dame: 108

**4  Haunted Libraries: 111**

Gorgas House and Gorgas Library—
   University of Alabama: 112

Hoskins Library—University of Tennessee: 114

Pattee Library—Penn State: 115

Memorial Library—University of Wisconsin: 117

Blegen Library—University of Cincinnati: 118

**5  Haunted Quads, Grounds, and Cemeteries: 121**

A Walk on the Wild Side: 121

The Haunted Quad—University of Alabama: 122

The Haunted Hill—University of Tennessee: 124

Agricultural Campus—University of Tennessee: 127

The Main Quadrangle—University of Illinois: 128

Eugene Pioneer Cemetery—University of Oregon: 130

**6  Theaters, Music Buildings,
   and Performance Halls: 133**

The Ghosts Must Go On: 133

Gallaway Theatre—University of Alabama: 134

E. C. Mabie Theatre—University of Iowa: 135

Northrop Auditorium—
   University of Minnesota: 137

Schwab Auditorium—Penn State: 139

Wisconsin Union Theater —
   University of Wisconsin: 142

McGraw Tower—Cornell University: 143

Marroney Theatre—University of Arizona: 144

Fisher Theater—Iowa State University: 146

Purple Masque Theatre—Kansas State University: 147

Washington Hall—University of Notre Dame: 150

7 **Sororities and Fraternities: 155**

When "Hell Week" Lasts a Little Longer than
Expected…: 155

Kappa Delta, Alpha Omicron Pi, Delta Tau Delta—
University of Maryland: 156

Sigma Alpha Epsilon—University of Oregon: 158

Sigma Phi Epsilon—Iowa State University: 159

Greek Ghosts—University of Ohio: 160

8 **Haunted People and Things: 165**

Guthrie Theater—Ghost of a
University of Minnesota Student: 166

Ezra Cornell's Family—Cornell University: 168

Hiram Corson—Cornell University: 169

General John Sedgwick—West Point: 170

Lieutenant Sutton's Spirit—U.S. Naval Academy: 171

The Ghost of John Paul Jones—
U.S. Naval Academy: 173

The Fighting Illini's Haunted Elevators—
University of Illinois: 175

Washington Avenue Bridge—
University of Minnesota: 179

Bascom Hill—University of Wisconsin: 181

Uris Hall—Cornell University: 183

The Cincinnati Observatory Center—
University of Cincinnati: 184

Duke Chapel—Duke University: 186

Rossborough Inn—University of Maryland: 187

**9  Off-Campus Haunts: 191**

School Spirits Found in Off-Campus Locations: 191

Ghostess with the Mostess and other Iowa City
Ghost Stories: 192

McCall Hall—University of Minnesota–Crookston: 196

Haunted Branch Campuses—
University of Pittsburgh: 197

*Afterword: Are Universities Really Haunted?: 211*

*Bibliography: 215*

# Introduction

## A Lesson in the Paranormal

There you are. A late-night study session turned into an early morning study session at the campus library, an old—even ancient—building located at the far end of a tree-lined quad, an immaculate lawn bordered by buildings that are just as old, just as historic. Just as creepy.

The library is deserted, you notice, as you carefully navigate through the stacks and stacks of books. But just as you turn the corner of the last row of books and with the freedom of the library's exit plainly in sight, you get the feeling you are not alone. A cold chill sizzles down your spine. Then, you hear a noise. When you turn around, you see—at least you think you see—a shadow creeping around the reference section.

Eye strain?

Too much caffeine?

Or a ghost.

Picture yourself. You come back to your dorm room from a night on the town. You notice that things seem askew. Books are spread out across the floor. It appears that the pencils and pens that you kept in the Go State coffee mug have exploded onto your desk. You know who the prime suspect is: your roommate. But as you sit down to contemplate possible revenge scenarios, the lights flicker. The television instantly turns on—and you're nowhere near the remote.

A practical joke?

Electromagnetic interference?

Bad wiring?

Or a poltergeist.

Imagine. You're back visiting the old digs of your alma mater. It's late evening on a football Saturday night. You decide to cut across the small grove of trees that border the campus. The once-vibrant red and orange leaves have turned crisp and brown on the ground and hiss and crackle under your feet as you trudge along. You forgot that a cemetery that contains the graves of the school's founders rests right on your path. That's exactly when you see it—a flittering silver shape hugging an obelisk gravestone.

Was it your imagination?

Excessive tailgating?

Or was it an actual encounter with an apparition?

Welcome to Paranormal 101—a class that is always in session in most university campuses across the nation and around the world. These institutions of higher education are the most haunted parcels of real estate, far outstripping even battlefields, cemeteries, and castles on a ghost story-by-ghost story basis.

In this book, we'll go across the country and visit some of the most haunted campuses and their most haunted buildings. You will get a peek—if you're not too afraid to look—at why campuses are so haunted. The natural and supernatural exist at colleges and universities, places where science has supposedly vanquished the paranormal into the corner cobwebs of history.

Campuses are like little villages with buildings set aside for specific uses. Every part of the student's spiritual, athletic, academic, and social life has its place on campus, and this book is divided into those campus building types. For instance, there is a section on residence halls and dormitories, a particularly spooky place for a college student. And I'm not even referring to your roommate's hygiene habits.

You'll explore haunted libraries, too. Most paranormal experts say that spirits seem drawn to the tight corridors of bookshelves and cavernous reading rooms in collegiate libraries.

Some universities have been the scene of more than Saturday gridiron battles. As the American Civil War violently ripped apart the country, once idyllic college campuses became contested ground in epic battles. The tremendous psychic energy generated by those terrifying events, paranormal researchers say, has imprinted spirits onto the very soil of those schools. Cemeteries and the graves of school leaders and founders also add to the haunted lore of college campuses.

Student thespians are used to suspending reality for their audiences, but in some theaters reality is suspended permanently. We'll visit haunted theaters and music halls where beautiful music is accompanied by the occasional bump in the night and moan of lost spirits.

The socials at sororities and fraternities on some college campuses include more than a couple drunken revelers. Spirits—not the kind found in the punch bowl—are present, too.

And there are more places to visit. Campus ghosts lurk in every type of building. From churches to museums, from the center of campus to far reaches of the school's host towns, ghosts wander, poltergeists prank, and apparitions appear.

Listen.

The bells on the quad are chiming.

Paranormal 101 is in session.

Take your seat.

# Disclaimer

Many university ghost stories are based on real people. In folklore and ghost lore, fact and fiction are easily blended. The circumstances of the lives and deaths of many people who figure prominently in ghost stories cannot be verified and it is difficult to determine the actual causes of paranormal activity. Stories in this book should not always be considered historical accounts, but are an accurate interpretation of the folklore and oral traditions that surround the events of their lives.

Ghost hunting is fun, but only when it is safe and permitted. Check first to make sure your explorations are allowed by the college or university, or ask for permission. Make sure the places you visit are safe and don't go alone. Some universities in this book actually embrace their ghostly roots and host tours and hunts on their own. That's probably the safest and best way to ghost hunt.

# 1

# STUDENT UNION BUILDINGS AND STUDENT CENTERS

Student union buildings and student centers are hot spots for activities outside of the realm of everyday studies and sports that consume the days and nights of your typical college student. They are places to grab a quick bite at one of the restaurants in the cafeteria or snack on munchies from the vending machine. They are places to shoot a game of pool or listen to music. You'll always find a few students curled up on comfy chairs to chat or catch up on the daily assigned readings.

But in some schools, student unions aren't just the center of student activity; they're the center of supernatural activity.

Ghost stories that take place in these hubs are extensive. The reasons behind the appearance of ghosts and spirits are just as vast. In the next few stories, we'll discover that former students may be the cause of these haunted student hubs. Founders and departed prominent university figures may also still roam the halls in spirit form. But, the source of these hauntings may be inhuman. Objects and artifacts appear to play a role in the supernatural activity.

Our first stop is at the Big Ten's Indiana University, home of the Hoosiers and home of one of the most haunted student centers—the Indiana Memorial Union.

## Indiana Memorial Union—Indiana University
### *Ghosts Make a Federal Case of IMU*

With its restaurants, theater, and even a bowling alley, Indiana Memorial Union—the Hoosier Nation just calls it IMU—has become not just the center for student life at the university; it appears that it has become the center of student afterlife, too.

The 90-year-old IMU has more than 500,000 square feet of space, giving the place both plenty of history and more than enough room for a few ghosts and poltergeists.

In an interview with the *Indiana Daily Student*, Melanie Hunter, a member of the Bloomington chapter of Indiana Ghost Trackers, said paranormal researchers have gathered lots of evidence that the building is haunted.

"The Union is full of paranormal activity," Hunter told the paper. "It pretty much runs the gamut of experience from auditory and visual disturbances to power drainage."

One of the hottest paranormal spots in IMU is the Federal Room, a stately space with ornate wallpaper depicting scenes of everyday life in nineteenth-century Indiana. Visitors say there's something strange about the wallpaper that they just can't quite put their finger on.

It's almost like the men and women portrayed on the wall scene are—somehow—alive.

The Federal Room would be just another room on campus—albeit a room slightly on the ostentatious side—if not for the interesting choice of wallpaper and the long line of witnesses who claim to have seen the filmy apparition of a woman wandering around.

Folks who have encountered the spirit of the Federal Room have a unique interpretation of the encounter. They swear the ghost looks exactly like one of the characters from the wallpaper. After all, the ghost that haunts the halls of the IMU is dressed from the time period depicted in the art.

Maybe this two-dimensional entity just got tired of hanging around —literally.

There's another, more disturbing, artistic legend. Some people claim that the female spirit is from one of the paintings that hangs in the Federal Room. There's a legend that the unfinished painting of university dignitary Mary Burney has something to do with the haunting. Mary apparently didn't like the portrait—and that's the reason why the work remains incomplete.

The fact that the university administrators went ahead and hung the painting that she detested continues to haunt the Federal Room. According to the student newspaper, the *Indiana Daily Student*, experts believe Mary is also behind the sudden and dramatic changes in temperature in the room, too.

The legend gets even stranger. According to the tale, Mary, her husband, and son died in a fire. An urn containing the ashes of Mary's husband and son were placed next to the unfinished painting. But they mysteriously vanished. No one has ever been able to find them.

Could it be that it's Mary who haunts the Federal Room, still in search of those missing remains? Possibly.

Or, could she just be looking for an artist to finish that dang painting?

As far as auditory phenomena (paranormal evidence that you can hear), Hunter said that people have heard children laughing and the sound of bouncing balls throughout the building.

Employees frequently say they have heard children playing.

But it's not all fun and games in haunted IMU. There's some real paranormal action.

There are reports of poltergeist activities on the top floor of IMU. It's there that some unseen spirit or entity has caused objects to move and vibrate. Every once in a while, the poltergeist seems to be unable to keep its hands—or claws—off of the lights. The lights will turn off unexpectedly, only to be turned on again.

Sometimes you can almost detect a pattern for the strange light show.

Once, one former student reported that while he was on the top floor, the lights went completely out. Bathed in the complete darkness, he struggled to find the light switch. As his fingers slowly felt the switch almost in his grasp, the lights immediately turned on again. The student turned and began to walk away when the lights flickered and then turned completely out. He again struggled to find the switch and, just as he did, you guessed it: on came the lights.

After a few rounds of this otherworldly teasing, the student bid a hasty retreat from IMU. Even though he returned to IMU, the student claims he never went to the top floor again.

The Tudor Room, one of IMU's dining spots, has a similar spirit. The ghost of a boy reportedly haunts the room.

A picture of a boy in the Tudor Room appears to be the focus of the activity. Legend has it that the boy died in a fire, just as Mary Burney's husband and child did.

Initially, the spirit was shy and the phenomena was minor.

Then, someone got the idea to take down the antique tapestries and have them cleaned. The spirit went wild and took his displeasure out on the staff of the Tudor Room. His activity since then has been "moody," at best.

But, it's a safe bet the cleaning crew thinks twice before they take down the tapestries for a good washing.

### ENCOUNTERS IN THE MAPLE ROOM

The Maple Room, located on the sixth floor, is another paranormal hot spot at IMU. The accounts don't just come from hyper students and urban legend buffs; the stories often come from the most reliable witness who have the most experience in IMU—the staff who work there every day and—for the more intrepid employees—every night.

"Supposedly a guy named Arthur Metz donated a lot of money when they were first building the Union," said Josh Olson, an IMU employee. "One stipulation was that he would have his own apartment and get to live on the sixth floor in what's called the Maple Room. He died right before the building was finished and is supposedly still up there."

Indiana University graduate student Dan Peretti has also heard of other creepy happenings in the Maple Room.

"I've talked to Union staff who swear that the Maple Room and the Student Activities Tower in general are haunted," Peretti said. "One person claimed that after turning the lights of the Maple Room off, he would notice them back on after leaving the building."

One night, after turning off the lights a third time, the staff member saw the reflection of a man standing behind him in a window. The ghost freaked out and ran away through the wall.

Melanie Hunter, secretary of the Bloomington chapter of Indiana Ghost Trackers, a group that attempts to "hunt" ghosts in southern Indiana, is familiar with the IMU folklore.

"The Union is full of paranormal activity," she said. "It pretty much runs the gamut of experience from auditory and visual disturbances to power drainage."

Hunter said the Bryan Room smells like old cigars even though nobody can smoke up there.

"You get the feeling of being watched," she said.

Hunter said it is common for people to hear children's laughter and the bouncing of balls throughout the IMU. Like a good philosophy lecture, the IMU hides more than it reveals. Are the sounds of children related to Mary Burney's ghost? Is it caused by Arthur Metz, the permanent resident of the building? Could there be other ghosts in the building? Who is behind this haunting?

It's not the only place on the Indiana University campus that there are hundreds of questions for each answer. La Casa next is the cultural center for Latino students and a supernatural center for those who believe that ghosts stalk the halls and quads of American universities.

## La Casa,
## Latino Cultural Center—Indiana University
*Who Ya Gonna Call? El Fantasma Busters?*

In Spanish, it's *el fantasma*—the ghost. According to many people, La Casa, Indiana University's Latino Cultural Center, has at least one fantasma—maybe more.

The center, a cozy-looking building nestled in a shady grove on the southern edge of campus on East Seventh Street, is a friendly-enough looking hacienda-away-from-hacienda for the college's Latino community. It's a great hangout to reconnect with the community.

Some students and visitors have noticed another member of the college's spiritual community hanging around La Casa. A woman has been seen walking around the building's upstairs by more than a few witnesses.

Typically, these encounters go like this: the figure of a woman moves along the halls and rounds a corner. Then, a curious—and brave—student decides to trail after the woman to find out who the stranger is. Just as she turns the same corner that the woman rounded just seconds before, the intrepid ghostbuster finds that the lady is gone. She vanished.

Most campus ghost tales have a backstory, some type of explanation of who is haunting the building and maybe even why they're still trapped in between the realms of the living and the dead.

This story is peculiar, then. There's no indication who this lost senorita is. Her story and the reason why she continues to haunt the Latino Cultural Center remains a mystery.

## O' Connell House—Boston College
### *BC's Student Paranormal Activity House*

When students at Boston College want to hang out, they go to the O'Connell House. When ghosts want to haunt students, they hang out at the O'Connell House.

BC's most famous residence was once owned by the drugstore baron Louis K. Liggett, who lived there until 1937. Cardinal William O'Connell, class of 1881, donated it to the university, along with nine acres. Lorraine Warren, one of the world's preeminent paranormal researchers, said that the property has a number of ghosts, including two women, a baby...and a dog.

"What can I say, I'm an animal lover," she said to students during a talk about her findings.

Warren's encounter with the spirit of the pooch has been confirmed. Students say they have seen a dog in the building.

Feven Teklu, a former student manager at the O'Connell House, told the *Heights*, BC's student newspaper, that the ghost dog is just one of the mysteries she's encountered while working there.

"Every now and then I'll be lying in bed and see this little dog sitting under my desk looking at me," said Teklu. "It's there, and then it disappears. It's kind of eerie and definitely a mystery."

Before you ask, Teklu added that neither she, nor her fellow managers at the time, owned a dog.

There are more strange encounters at the O'Connell.

On a few occasions, a hair dryer has turned on by itself. Lights turn on and off without anyone even being near the switches, and blinds draw themselves close.

Students also report feeling a presence—perhaps the presence of one of the spirits that paranormal reseacher Lorraine Warren detected in the building.

So who—or what—is behind the O'Connell House haunting?

Since most haunted houses are scenes of highly emotional incidents or tragic events, we would suspect that highly charged activities at the 32,007-square-foot O'Connell House must be the root cause of the haunting.

Sort of.

At least for the last 30 or so years, the building has served as the site of special BC events like the Middlemarch Ball and Harvest Nights, as well as a lot of band concerts. Formal dances and rock concerts may have generated their share of bad dance moves and breakup dramas. But could this energy have generated the paranormal activity that haunts the O'Connell?

The O'Connell House's exquisite Tudor architecture and large gardens attracted Hollywood directors. Portions of *13 Rue Madeleine*, a movie starring James Cagney, were filmed in the house. The crew never seemed to report any strange activity during filming, though.

What about the great drugstore king, Mr. Liggett? Paranormal researchers suggest that the death of Liggett's wife, Musa, in 1931 prompted Liggett to donate the home to Cardinal O'Connell. Did his wife's death make the big mansion empty, except for the memories of a fonder time? Or did the haunting activity cause the drugstore baron to donate the place to the church in the first place? Unfortunately, no one knows the answers. At best, they're only a few of the theories that surround BC's house of mystery.

Skeptics suggest the haunting of O'Connell isn't related to the spirits of dead students, faculty members, founders, celebrities, or even the wife of a drugstore baron. The haunting is just another campus legend, the higher education version of urban legends like the phantom hitchhiker or the hook-handed killer. Disregarding testimonials from witnesses like Teklu, skeptics believe that the tales of ghosts in O'Connell are spread from student to student and from class to class until they take on a life of their own.

Not so fast, say believers, or at least those open-minded enough to consider supernatural explanations.

Joseph Tecce, a BC psychology professor, told the newspaper that he keeps an open mind about paranormal accounts at O'Connell House.

"The O'Connell House mystery should be treated as such—a mystery without a definitive explanation and a mystery that can be discussed and investigated," Tecce said. "Many phenomena occur in our lives for which we don't have a clear explanation. To accept extrasensory phenomena as feasible, we should exhaust all the possible natural and logical explanations and then entertain possible reasons that go beyond the natural and scientific levels of discourse."

## Willard Straight Hall—Cornell University
### *Former Students Make Formal Spirits*

Willard Straight Hall is the student union located in central campus of Cornell University. It's also plays a central role in Corneliana—the list of unique Cornell customs, traditions, and legends.

According to experts of Corneliana, the widow of Willard Straight was desperate to make contact with her departed husband. Willard was an investment banker and Cornell grad. When he passed away, his wife, Dorothy, contributed a substantial amount of money to have the student union center built.

This wasn't the only way Dorothy tried to keep her husband's spirit alive. She continued to try to contact her beloved husband from beyond the grave. According to some stories, she tried to reach Willard during seances. No one's sure if she was successful, but the contact with the spirit world appears to have taken hold in Willard Straight Hall.

Witnesses have seen men in tuxedos, dressed like they're going to formal party, walking around the student union. A maid, now long-since retired, said she, too, came into contact with a young man in a tuxedo.

Sure, there are still formal affairs at Cornell. But the men described in the encounters appear to be from a different age. The tuxedos are of a different style. The hairstyles are out-of-date, too.

For those who have seen the fleeting glimpse of the tuxedoed Cornell gents, there's no doubt who they are. They're ghosts.

## Healy Hall— Georgetown University

### *Can School Spirits Be Exorcised?*

With all the spirits stalking the capital and Georgetown, tales of haunted spots invariably return to Healy Hall, Georgetown University's entry into the realms of Washington D.C.'s legends.

It's a picture perfect spot for a haunting.

The structure is a massive, regal-looking building built by the same architects who designed the Library of Congress. Named after the nation's first black university president, Patrick Healy, the building currently contains the office of the president, the Kennedy Institute of Ethics, the Riggs Library, and several other offices and societies. Healy also houses historic Gaston Hall, a grand 750-seat auditorium that is perhaps the most famous space on the Georgetown campus.

The building also served as living quarters for students and teachers, according to some Georgetown folklore experts.

Also worthy of note: Georgetown's Philodemic Society, one of the oldest college debating clubs, meets in the Philodemic Room at Healy Hall. While there's no record the Philodemic Society ever tackled the subject, there is definitely one subject that's continually debated by Georgetown students: is Healy Hall haunted?

The argument has nothing to do with the continual and mysterious disappearance of the building's world-famous clock hands. It had been a rite of passage for students to risk death by scaling the clock tower, stealing the hands, and then mailing them to the Vatican.

Advocates of the "Healy is haunted" position say the evidence rises above the level of college pranks. Something sinister is going on here. As proof, they cite a story that has passed through the student body like accounts of the basketball prowess of Patrick Ewing and other Hoya basketball legends. The legend begins with a Jesuit priest who lived on the fifth floor. While other students may complain about completing Stat assignments and studying for Calculus finals, word had it that the priest had some heavy-duty homework. He was deeply involved in studying archaic tracts on how to defeat evil. The ancient texts covered everything from battling demons to exorcising evil spirits.

In the properly trained and schooled hands of a Jesuit, this knowledge served as tools and weapons to defeat demons. But in the hands of less-experienced spiritual warriors, these texts could be satanic traps designed to ensnare souls.

As it happened, the Jesuit's apprentice entered the priest's room one day. In a moment of carelessness, the priest had forgotten to stash the books away. The apprentice began to read some of the esoteric verses. Worse, he began to read the verses aloud.

When the Jesuit heard the commotion, he ran to his room. But it was too late.

The apprentice had opened up a portal to hell on the fifth floor of Healy Hall!

The evil spirits have had the run of the place since.

So, is it a true story? Or is it a great campus legend, albeit with the splendid Catholic twist that Georgetown students would love?

The debate rages.

Some say they have experienced unexplainable events while on the fifth floor of Healy. Flickering lights, moving objects, and shifting temperatures that convinced them that there may be truth to the story of the Jesuit's apprentice. Others say the only evil spirits were the pranksters who stole the hands from Healy Hall's famous clock tower.

## The Dining Hall and Other Fighting Irish Ghosts—University of Notre Dame

*A Tour of More Haunted Spots at Notre Dame*

Bryce Chung is no stranger to the paranormal. He told *Notre Dame Magazine* that his home in Hawaii, a land imbued with ancestral spirits and supernatural superstitions, was haunted. He saw something climbing up and down the steps in his home and sometimes caught the reflection of someone in his computer monitor as he played video games.

Later, his neighbor told Chung that the spirit that haunted his home was probably his grandfather's.

When Chung traveled to study chemical engineering and business at the University of Notre Dame, he initially thought that he left the world of ancestral spirits back in the mystical islands of Hawaii. He didn't experience any paranormal phenomena—not during late-night walks between buildings, not in the nearby cemeteries, not in his living quarters.

Nothing.

Then he went to work at a popular eatery in the South Dining Hall. One of his jobs was to restock the shelves in the basement of the diner. While he worked, that familiar feeling that he wasn't alone returned. He sensed a presence.

In another encounter, Chung said that while working in the basement, a radio suddenly turned on.

Intrigued, Chung asked his coworkers if they ever sensed anything supernatural in the dining hall. The stories gushed out of the staff.

Some employees heard strange noises—like clapping and moans.

Other people told him that they saw bizarre reflections that flash in the stainless steel of the kitchen equipment.

Another employee offered the most fantastic tale. She said that one morning—around 4 a.m.—she turned to see a white figure floating outside the dining room doors! Later, when the employee saw a picture hanging above a fireplace she positively identified the ghost she saw on the early morning shift.

It was Father Sorin, a well-known Notre Dame figure.

Chung was so fascinated by the ghost stories that he started to offer a haunted tour of the Notre Dame campus, a tour that covered Washington Hall's spooky history, the ghosts of Main Hall, Father Sorin's apparitions, and, of course, his own experiences in the South Dining Hall.

What's the secret of Notre Dame's haunting? Chung has a few theories based on his own studies of engineering and neurology:

"I actually think [ghosts are] a manifestation of our brain. At the same time, though, there are bits and pieces that are left unexplained by that approach. So I guess you could say I leave space for something greater."

# 2

# DORMITORIES AND RESIDENCE HALLS

## Rooming with the Paranormal

For millions of college students, the dormitory becomes more than a convenient place that's close to class; it's a home away from home and the people who live there become a family away.

The resident assistants or resident advisors—better known as RAs—who watch over a floor of college kids are often seen as parental figures by new students. Roommates almost become siblings, for better or worse. Fellow students who live on the same floor and in the rest of the dorm fill out the rest of this temporary, but important, extended family.

There's one more comparison. The dormitory is not immune to spirits and ghosts that can stalk the typical family home. In fact, if students expect to escape the paranormal by moving into a dorm room, they're in for a surprise. Dorms are among the most haunted structures on campus.

In the next few pages, we'll delve into the stories of paranormal activity that have been recorded at university dorms and residence halls across the nation. The activity is a veritable menu of supernatural events. Active spirits, residual spirits, poltergeists, and malicious entities seem to wait in each hall, in each room, and in each common area.

Dorm hauntings have a range of causes.

Tragedy and death can strike the youngest and most vulnerable. Untimely deaths and suicides play a role in tales of dorm hauntings. The ghosts of university founders also pay visits to students who live in the dorms. Finally, paranormal research experts say that pulling young people—who are filled with excitement and nervous energy—together can result in a crescendo of psychic energy that is released through poltergeist-type activity.

Our tour of haunted dorms starts in Strong Hall, the University of Tennessee's most haunted dorm.

## Strong Hall—University of Tennessee
*Strong Vibes Felt throughout Residence Hall*

Strong Hall was once the beloved residence hall for the University of Tennessee's female students.

The hall was named after Sophorina Strong, daughter of wealthy magnate Benjamin Rush Strong who left the university a sizable dona-tion. He never could have known that the spirit of his daughter would be among the contributions left to the dormitory.

Though it closed as a residence hall in 2008, the long history of the building notched up a long record of spirit sightings and haunted hap-penings. Most students attributed the ghostly events to Sophie, who died in 1867. Folklorists have a few theories why Sophie remained at Strong Hall. After years of living at the university and watching over the students, who came and went in methodical four-year increments, her spirit became deeply attached to the campus and its students. When she died, her spirit, like some indecisive grad students, stayed on.

Former resident assistant Beth Newman was among the students who had an incident or two to talk about after her stay at Strong Hall. Newman said she had an unusual welcome to Strong Hall. She said on the first day that she moved into her room, a pile of papers were blasted onto the floor.

She felt no breeze. The air conditioner wasn't on either.

Like most students, Newman knew who to blame: Sophie.

Sophie's manifestations aren't always as mischievous, nor are they as subtle. According to reports, students have witnessed apparitions of Sophie. The timing is interesting. Most reports filter in during times of conflict among the students, such as roommates fighting and friends who have just had an argument. Sophie's appearance seems to heal the rift. As a mother of 12 children during her earthly existence, Sophie's motherly qualities are undiminished in the afterlife.

One story of Sophie's maternal side, reported in *Mysterious Knoxville*, goes like this:

Two former residents of Strong Hall were having a discussion. The discussion turned into a debate. Then it morphed into an outright argument. The two women argued, their voices turned into screams, until one friend quickly became silent. The other student turned around just in time to see the ghost of Sophie standing in front of them. With her hands on her hips and a glare of disappointment on her face, Sophie appeared to be scolding them.

There's no report how the argument was settled, but you can bet it was ended amicably.

So, this is typical campus legend fare: ghost appears to enforce rules of behavior. But is there any evidence that the haunting is paranormal? A group of paranormal researchers—the East Tennessee Paranormal Research Society—conducted a study of Strong Hall and came away with some weird evidence. For instance, the portrait of Sophie that hangs in the hall was 20 degrees warmer than the rest of the building. Maybe Sophie has a temper? In addition to experiencing "major battery drain"—a sign that an unseen entity was drawing power from the environment—the team caught orbs flitting around the building's original stairwell on a video. Some say orbs and other phenomena that appear on videos and in photographs are spirits caught in the act.

Sophie isn't just a drama mama who appears during arguments. One more Strong Hall legend states that Sophie would appear on her birthday—February 17—if you looked in the large mirror that once dominated the main lobby of the dorm.

And students being students and never requiring an excuse to party, a tradition of throwing a birthday party for Sophie was soon started.

There's no report she ever showed up for the party-in-the-mirror birthday bash.

But, honestly, what Southern lady wants to be reminded she's pushing 200 years old?

## Read Hall Dormitory—Indiana University

*Read Hall ... or Dread Hall?*

Indiana University's Read Hall is the peculiar X-shaped co-educational dorm.

It's four wings are named Beck, Clark, Curry, and Landes. Male students reside in the Beck and Curry wings and women live in the Clark and Landes sections.

And ghosts reside all over the place.

Read Hall's "X" reportedly marks the spot of one of the most well-known haunted buildings on the campus of Indiana University.

The story of Read Hall begins with a lethal combination in college folklore: a pretty coed and a jealous boyfriend. In most renditions of this legend, the boyfriend, a premed student, was growing more and more suspicious of his girlfriend, a pretty thing known for her long black hair.

Eventually the suspicions turned into jealousy, and the jealousy turned into a homicidal rage.

The story continues that one night, using his skills in premed, he murdered his girlfriend in his dorm room.

According to one account, the boyfriend used a scalpel to slit her throat. In another account, it was the old reliable ax or a hatchet—a favorite of homicidal students destined to be urban legends. Whatever the instrument of the crime, all accounts agree that the boyfriend disposed of her body, with equal efficiency, in one of the tunnels beneath the building.

His crime didn't go unpunished—the boyfriend eventually confessed to police and led authorities to the body.

While the beautiful girl's body was removed, the spirit was, apparently, less than willing to be taken away.

Since the night of that dreadful crime, students have reported seeing a girl with long, dark hair wearing a yellow nightgown gliding through the halls at night or standing in the room where she was murdered. Her presence is most often seen on the top floors of the building. In some accounts, the murder occurred on the third floor, and in others, the sixth floor. Students indicate that the third floor seems to be the most active.

Just like so many elements of her story, the reason for the Ghost in Yellow's haunting vary. A common explanation is that the sheer trauma of the murder has trapped this girl in that filmy netherworld between planes of existence.

A less common, but more disturbing, version of this story indicates she isn't trapped at all. She just wants one thing … revenge.

## Currier Hall—University of Iowa

*Blessed Are the Peacemakers, Even When They're Dead*

Most grads will tell you that the best lessons they received during their college years weren't those taught by their professors and instructors. They received the most important life lessons living with and learning from their friends and classmates, especially their roommates and dormmates.

Study habits, spending tips, and even dating advice are passed on from friend to friend, student to student during your college years. And the bonds and connections you make at college can run deep enough to last a lifetime.

The students who room at Currier Hall don't need the reminder. They have some otherworldly instructors from beyond the grave to make sure they're learning the really important lessons.

According to the legend that has filtered down through the years, three female dormmates once resided in Currier Hall and they quickly became best friends. As it happened, each girl eventually became romantically involved with a new beau.

The girls were happy for each other. They seemed to have it all: great friendships, interesting classes, and, now, romance.

Until one day, when the roommates began to compare notes about their new boyfriend.

What started out as a review of silly similarities about the boys they fell in love with—same style of dress, same major, and probably even the same pickup line—suddenly turned into the stark revelation: the girls had fallen in love with the same boy.

None of the girls could live without him.

They arrived at a fateful, unfortunate decision. Rather than live apart from the man they loved and each other, they decided to die together.

Most of the tales pinpoint that this triple suicide occurred on the fourth floor. This is probably the reason that, if you stand outside Currier Hall today, you'll notice a few people glancing up warily at the haunted fourth floor, the top floor of this long, elegant building.

In most paranormal cases, suicides lead to negative and even malicious hauntings.

This doesn't seem to be the case for the Currier Hall haunting. Witnesses say that the spirits of the girls now appear as a warning anytime friends have disagreements. It's their way of emphasizing the real lesson for the feuding friends: boys come and go, but friendships should last forever.

Currier Hall's other spirits aren't all pleasant and helpful, students say. Another legend about the dorm is that it's haunted by the father of a former resident.

A man, whose face is etched with concern and worry, appears in the E 300 section of Currier Hall. His apparition has been seen wandering through the section. Some students say he's the father of one of the suicide victims; others say he has nothing to do with that story.

He does seem linked to other poltergeist-type activities in the building. Residents complain of televisions that inexplicably turn on and off, and closet doors that open and close by themselves.

Some residents of the dorm speculate that this activity could be the ghost of a worried parent saying to the students: "Quit watching television . . . and are you really wearing that out in public?"

For a campus that isn't exactly urban, the University of Iowa sure has a lot of urban legends.

## Slater Hall—University of Iowa

*Home of the Urban Legend—Iowa Style*

Situated at the west end of the University of Iowa's campus, Slater Hall looks like a typical college dormitory. It's close to the university's famous Pentacrest and the sports campus. The building has healthy lifestyle floors and a quiet floor. And, if rumors are to be believed, it has a few angry spirits who are looking to lop off students' heads and dine on their carcasses.

So much for the healthy lifestyle floor.

But that is, indeed, the strange reputation that hangs over the dorm named after the legendary Hawkeye's football player, Fred "Duke" Slater. According to tales passed on from student to student, a former tenant of the building decided, much like his female classmates across campus at Currier Hall, that college life was too much for him and plummeted from the ninth floor of Slater.

Unlike his fellow University of Iowa suicide victims in Currier, he has no intention of serving as a positive influence on the living residents of Slater. He has no desire to patch up friendships that may be under stress. In fact, students say they see the ghost of a young man walking the halls, normally late at night or early in the morning, carrying an ax.

Witnesses don't think the ghost is trying to help out Iowa's landscaping crew, and they don't hang around to ask what he's up to. They say the Slater Hall spirit is bound to avenge his suicide by taking someone else's life—rather than his own—this time.

If one crazed spirit isn't enough, there's also mention of a "Penguin man" who isn't interested in merely a head—he wants to eat students whole.

For paranormal investigators, these stories smack of good old-fashioned college urban legend, with a little surreal humor tossed in.

In the end, maybe the ghost of the ax-wielding maniac and the carnivorous Penguin man do play a positive role. At least resident hall administrators don't have to worry about their charges wandering around Slater Hall late at night.

## Pioneer Hall—University of Minnesota

### *Superhaunt in the Superblock*

Pioneer Hall is one of the four residence halls on the campus's East Bank that forms an area called the Superblock. Since the Superblock is a collection of dorms and dining facilities, it's a popular area for students and hosts a lot of social activities.

Unfortunately, it's also, according to some, superhaunted.

Pioneer Hall, which houses about 700 students, looks the part of a haunted dorm—the old-world charm of its exterior and narrow interior with stark, barren halls and tunnels give it a foreboding feel, like an old hospital or an asylum.

There's a campus legend that states that Anneliese Michel lived in Pioneer Hall during the exorcism that was portrayed in the movie *The Exorcism of Emily Rose*. There's a slight problem with that. Oh, heck, who am I kidding? There's a lot wrong with that.

Anneliese was a German girl and went to a German university. The American movie was drastically altered from the original version of her story.

But, there are other stories that are harder to disprove.

One student legend indicates that Pioneer Hall has more than the "feel" of a hospital—it's an accurate assessment of the building's early function. According to the legend, the building was once used as a makeshift insane asylum and patients from nearby Fairview Hospital were housed in Pioneer Hall. The legend goes on to say that one of the patients, a mentally ill girl, never left. She still haunts the halls.

Witnesses report strange noises and voices carrying through the building's narrow passageways. When students close in on the noises, they disappear.

There isn't any research to suggest that the hall was a temporary asylum. (Of course, if you visit Pioneer Hall on a Friday or Saturday night, you might not be so sure.) But the legend of ghosts of insane people seem to serve at least one purpose: scare the bejeezers out of first-year students.

## Sanford Hall—University of Minnesota

*Hear Her Roar…*

Most people would, without hesitation, say that the spirit of Maria Sanford can be felt on the campus of the University of Minnesota. Whether her spirit can be seen is another matter altogether.

In the late 1800s, when most women were confined to the narrowest of occupational opportunities, Maria Sanford dared to break the mold. She used her dowry to earn an education and entered the teaching profession. Gradually, she earned the respect of her peers on a state and then national level. Her career led her to Chester County, Pennsylvania (as a school superintendent), to Swarthmore College (as a history professor), and finally to the University of Minnesota, where she served as a professor in speech and a lecturer in, among other subjects, history. In her spare time, she championed women's rights, pioneered adult education, and gave hundreds of speeches.

She was a bit of an overachiever, and if her statue is any indication, she probably expected the same from her students.

A bust of Maria, tucked away in a recess of Sanford Hall, a residence hall that was named after her in 1910, offers a stern, piercing gaze from this pioneer in education. A statue of professor Sanford that was donated to the National Statuary Hall Collection also reveals a severe-looking matron.

Let's just say she looks like she had a strict attendance policy.

Students claim that Maria's spirit continues to roam through Sanford Hall. What she's looking for is anyone's guess. The consensus is she's trying to find a female student who isn't living up to her scholastic potential.

## Watts Hall—Penn State

### *Go to the Light, Coaly*

Penn State—once called the Farmer's High School—has blossomed since the days when it was reserved almost exclusively for agricultural education. It's no longer just a school for farmers. However, barns and silos—and the occasional roaming herd of livestock—serve as a reminder that Penn State maintains its reputation as a premier agricultural school.

There are, however, apparently more than cows, sheep, and goats that graze these lush hills and pastures. There's one animal in particular that, despite having been put out to pasture—way, way out to pasture —keeps returning to roam the grounds once more. Penn State is the only campus in the nation that is haunted by a mule.

Back in 1857, Coaly the mule was responsible for lugging cart after cart of stones to the site of the Farmer's High School, which eventually became Pennsylvania State University. He had the added duty of serving as Penn State's first mascot.

Old Coaly was so beloved by the students and faculty of this pioneering college that, when he finally laid his labors to rest in 1893, he was stuffed and displayed in a series of buildings throughout the campus. He had an extended stay at Watts Hall, a dormitory where he roomed with the remains of Penn State's current mascot, the Nittany Lion. Coaly's indomitable spirit apparently lives on there, some say.

Over the years, several reports have trickled out from the dorm that indicates that Coaly is still making his hard-working presence known. Students have been roused from their study sessions and their slumber and heaven knows what else when his mournful "hee-haw" echoes down the halls in the middle of the night.

There have also been stories about Old Coaly's silent and solemn strolls.

Students and dorm visitors say on some nights, perhaps when Coaly isn't feeling so vocal, you can hear the plodding of hooves echoing as the never-say-quit spirit of Coaly continues his journey down the dark corridors of the dormitory.

Of course, since good pranks are often as coveted as national football championships on college campuses, many victims of Coaly hauntings suspect practical jokers. But when they investigate, there's no sign of human intervention—no slamming doors, no footsteps, and not even rumors that the events were staged. And, as most know, pulling a prank is easy; keeping it secret is an entirely different matter.

Could it be that practical jokers aren't behind these stories, and maybe, a simpler explanation is that Old Coaly is just too stubborn to head to the light?

In other dorms in Penn State, it's not stubborn spirits that residents have to worry about—it's mischievous and sometimes downright evil poltergeists.

# Runkle Hall—Penn State

*Poltergeist 101*

The word, poltergeist, is German for "noisy spirit."

But the idea that there exists some kind of psychic energy that can disturb reality is universal—and ancient. The Romans have stories of poltergeist activity.

Paranormal researchers blame poltergeists for ghostly manifestations that are more like a drunken frat boy than a spirit. Poltergeists enjoy whooping it up—tossing books, breaking dishes, and slamming doors.

It could be that the poltergeist isn't a ghost or spirit at all, but a form of telekinesis, or "mind over matter," generated by a frustrated, but very much alive, human. Since there's lots of frustration and pent-up psychic energy in the typical college student, you might think that a university campus would make an ideal setting for a poltergeist outbreak.

You'd be right.

All you have to do is ask the occupants and resident administrators who encountered what they referred to as the poltergeist of Runkle Hall back in the 1990s. Runkle Hall is a peculiar L-shaped building in a collection of dormitories at the northern edge of campus collectively called North Halls.

It's always tough to figure out when poltergeist activity begins for a couple of reasons. First, the manifestations can be easily attributed to normal human-inspired pranks and natural occurring phenomena. The second reason is the activity starts out small and gradually builds into a crescendo of outrageous, and sometimes violent, displays. Those are both true of the poltergeist outbreak at Runkle. However, there were rumors of something strange going on in Runkle Hall for years.

While it may be impossible to nail down the actual start of the troubles at this Penn State dorm, the poltergeist activities hit a terrifying peak in the early- to mid-1990s. In 1992, the events seemed to center on one room—room 318—and on one girl. The subject of the haunting wasn't just an average student who may have had a little too much at an end-of-week mixer. According to reports from the *Daily Collegian*, the school's newspaper, the victim wasn't just a typical student; she was the floor's resident administrator.

A loud banging kept the RA up one night—a loud banging that seemed to have no explainable source. She said it sounded like someone was pounding a hammer, or fists, into the wall with alarming ferocity.

Her bed started to heave in and out as if it were breathing. The banging became increasingly more violent. There were electrical disturbances, too—lights flickered on and off.

Then the really weird stuff began to happen. Objects moved or disappeared altogether.

Finally, the RA had enough. She fled the room with friends, who also witnessed the poltergeist activity. When they returned to her room, she was locked out.

Six years later, another student was driven out of room 318.

This student said that she could hear strange mumbling—like someone speaking a foreign language—that seemed to be coming from within the walls.

In some respects, the reports of this haunting mirrored the events of the first poltergeist case. Items moved—or were hurled. Lights would flicker on and off, for instance.

Then there was the pounding again. The student told dorm leaders and fellow students that someone—or something—was pounding the walls violently.

It finally became so bad that she asked to be reassigned to new student housing. The poltergeist, content with the havoc that ensued, didn't seem inclined to follow her.

Campus authorities investigated the incident but never arrived at a satisfactory explanation. Those more inclined to things paranormal did come up with a few explanations. Some suggested it was a poltergeist.

However, the Runkle entity doesn't easily fit into the strict definition of a poltergeist. Poltergeists seem to attach themselves around a human source, called an "agent." Many times the poltergeist activity revolves around a troubled, but stilted, teenager. Like a spiritual vandal, the poltergeist acts out when the teen can't. While most poltergeists appear during that subject's perilous journey between childhood and adulthood, known as puberty, it's not out of the realm of possibility that the rigors and stress of college life could cause a poltergeist to appear— as anyone who has had three finals on the same day can attest.

Here's another key difference: poltergeists don't seem to be attached to rooms or buildings the way the Runkle spirit does.

Others suggested the room was not a source of poltergeist activity, but was haunted by a ghost of a suicide victim. Despite these rumors, reports indicate that no one ever committed suicide in Runkle Hall, although a student did commit suicide in nearby Leete Hall, according to one newspaper article.

Whatever or whoever the source, the Runkle Poltergeist hasn't been heard from lately.

Poltergeists, it seems, like good soldiers, never die—they just fade away.

## Syme Residence Hall, Bragaw Residence Hall—North Carolina State
### *Doomed Dorms or Residence Halls of Rumors*

Residence hall administrators have seen some strange things at NC State. And, if a few reports are true, it's not just the antics of those living in the dorms that concern NC State RAs; they have to watch out for the dead, too.

One RA at Syme Residence Hall told her charges that she had an encounter of the creepy kind on move-out day—that's the day when students vacate the dorm at the end of the semesters.

She said that the dorm was empty. Completely empty. But there was an odd feeling. The place, which was once bustling with student activity, was now silent and still. Who knows why the RA stuck around? Maybe she was just making sure the rooms were empty and the doors were locked.

The doors were all locked. But the rooms were far from empty.

As she finished her rounds, the RA came face-to-face with a ghost. She saw a young girl, about 10 to 13 years old, in the hall. A few things ran through her mind. The girl might be a sister of one of the former residents. Since she wasn't allowed in the dorm, the RA followed her. The girl moved down the hall, and the RA walked after her. The RA then watched the girl turn around a corner that was a dead end.

She, too, rounded the same corner expecting to confront the unexpected visitor. But she was gone.

The little girl—or more precisely, the little ghost—had disappeared.

NC State may have other paranormally active dorms.

Students at Bragaw Residence Hall say they have experienced strange activity, too. But there's no way of knowing whether this is related to the incidents at Syme. Nor are there any explanations of why the halls seem to attract the supernatural. There doesn't seem to be a death of a young girl that would account for the manifestation, though some speculate the apparition of the girl and other strange events might have something to do with the devastating influenza outbreak of 1918, which took the lives of 13 students.

The dorm spirits are one more NC State mystery.

## Thayer Hall—Harvard University
### *Harvard Yard's Most Haunted Address*

If any building on Harvard Yard (pronounced *Hah-vahd Yahd*) deserves to be haunted, it's Thayer Hall, one of the prestigious university's freshman dorms. Microsoft's Steve Ballmer and Prince Hamzah bin Al Hussein of Jordan once called Thayer Hall home. They reportedly shared Thayer with the ghosts of a group of mill employees who once worked in the building when it was used as a textile mill.

People claim to have seen misty apparitions drifting through the halls. For those who get a closer glimpse of the ghostly group, the spirits are dressed in Victorian-era garb, exactly how you would expect mill workers of that era to be dressed. The tale takes an even weirder turn—some of the workers appear to walk through the walls! Some people see the spirits outside walking into Thayer where there is no door. Those familiar with Thayer Hall say that some former entrances and exits were closed off when the building was reconditioned to become a dorm. If so, maybe the ghosts are traveling through the passageways that were once part of the mill, but have long since been closed off.

I know what you're thinking. You have an explanation for the Thayer ghost story. Since it's a freshman dorm, the ghosts are nothing more than the overactive imagination of a bunch of freshmen, or carefully constructed stories used to keep underclassmen from wandering the halls.

But, according to the *Harvard Crimson*, the student newspaper, it's not just freshmen who have witnessed the restless souls in Thayer. Paranormal researcher Fiona Broome said that a professor also saw ghosts in the building. He told Broome that the spirits appeared to pop in and out of walls.

"A professor who chose to remain anonymous contacted me and said that he had seen Victorian figures going through areas in the hall where there used to be doors and there aren't now," said Broome. "He had a lot of credibility. Just in the way that he wrote, I felt confident that this man was not a crazy person."

The best time to see the ghosts of Thayer is during the winter. For some reason, the workers are even more active when the cold Massachusetts winter sets in. However, the number of paranormal encounters has diminished over the years, especially since more artificial lighting is used outside. The new lighting may make it hard to discern the filmy presence of the workers, or it's driven the spirits out all together.

Then again, maybe these tough mill workers are just on break.

# Weld Hall—Harvard University

*Uncommon Presence in the Common Room*

Like every student who has ever stayed in Weld Hall, Audris Wong, a Harvard student in the mid-1980s, may have wondered about the spirits that haunt the Queen Anne–style dorm, built in 1870 as a gift from William Fletcher Weld.

Who knows? Maybe even on dark, stormy nights former Weld Hall resident John F. Kennedy mused about the possibility that shades of the afterworld were trapped in this historic building. As one of the first buildings in Harvard, the old residence hall was home away from home for a lot of young living souls. Perhaps, when their earthly matriculation was finished, some came back for an eternal semester.

Wong, however, didn't have to wonder very long. She saw the real thing.

In 1985—one of the darkest and stormiest nights in recent New England history—Hurricane Gloria had churned up the Atlantic seaboard, waxing and waning in strength like some type of malevolent spirit toying with the people who lived along the coast. The students, facing power outages, invested in some good old-fashioned candles.

Wong said she kept one of those candles—a red one—and decided to use it for an impromptu seance in her room.

The windows were open, letting the breeze and the muted light of the full moon mix in her North Weld room. The atmosphere from the room wasn't scary. Far from it. The student later told a reporter it was relaxing. But, that didn't last for long.

As Wong tells the story:

"My eyes were transfixed at the space between my two roommates, when I saw an old woman with a dark cloak and grayish hair. It wasn't like the mist that you see in the movies, but it was very vague—like an impression. I couldn't see any of her features. She was just leaning against the wall, listening to our conversation."

While her friends who attended the session didn't see the ghost (their backs were against the apparition), they did attest to Wong's encounter. They believed her.

Theresa M. McCarthy, who was there when Wong saw the spirit, said, "It was a really mellow atmosphere. Audris suddenly stopped the conversation and told us, in a calm voice, that the ghost was there."

And why wouldn't Wong have seen a ghost? There have been tales of ghosts and strange activity in Weld for years. One theory ties the ghosts of Weld to renovation work. Paranormal experts tell us that renovating an old building can unleash pent-up paranormal forces. According to one theory, after the building burned down in the 1960s, a massive restoration effort inadvertently walled in some spirits. Students say they have heard strange knocks that have echoed through the halls of the building ever since.

At least in this one case, though, some spirit at Weld decided to be seen and not heard.

## Haunted Houses—Harvard University
### *Why Upperclassmen Can't Escape the School's Ghostly Legacy*

Harvard's new arrivals bear the brunt of Harvard's haunted hazing. Freshmen are stuck in residence halls full of the departed souls of mill workers and apparitions of old women. If they think they'll escape the school's paranormal influence once they pass their freshman year, another chapter of the school's textbook hauntings lies waiting to be opened.

Harvard's famous "Houses," where Harvard's upperclassmen live, study, and hang out, have ghosts of their own; they might even have more ghosts than the freshman dorms. The House system is unique in American academics. A House isn't a single building; it's a collection of buildings. The system serves as an administrative subdivisions of Harvard and living quarters. (Think Gryffindoor, Slytherin, Hufflepuff, and Ravenclaw from the Harry Potter series.)

A senior faculty member, called a Master, presides over the House.

One house in particular—Adams House—is rumored to have the most ghosts.

Adams House is considered one of the most historic Houses. Adams was actually formed in 1931 as a collection of three former "Gold Coast" dormitories—Apthorp, Randolph, and Westmorly. The Houses once served as luxurious dorms for Harvard's upper-crust students, but were merged into Adams House as a way to end the social stratification that arose from the exclusive Gold Coast dorms.

Franklin Delano Roosevelt was a proud Adams House member. The House was also known for its artsy bent with actors Fred Gwynne, Peter Sellers, and John Lithgow among the artistic residents of Adams.

Somehow, lucky Adams House inherited a few ghosts, too.

Apthorp is the oldest House in Adams and is now the Master's Residence. Lots of students and residents also think it's one of the largest and most opulent structures in Cambridge. The building's notch in American history is significant. When the American Revolution tore through New England and Boston, specifically, Apthorp became a hot seat of Revolutionary activity. It's where Gen. Israel Putnam of the Continental Army planned the Battle of Bunker Hill.

When British general John Burgoyne, known as Gentleman Johnny, surrendered after the battle of Saratoga, he was held as a prisoner in Apthorp. He was not happy with the arrangements. There were few creature comforts, and the patriots even forced him to pay a steep rent.

Burgoyne's anger and frustration must have imprinted itself on the psychic fiber of Apthorp. The gentleman general and some other Revolutionary War soldiers are said to haunt the house.

One student who stayed in the attic of Apthorp claimed to hear evidence that the haunting was true.

"I hear them rumbling about all the time," said Hannah Bouldin, a student in the 1980s told the student newspaper. She even claimed that the spirit of General Borgoyne inspired a term paper.

If you're familiar with how General Burgoyne botched the Battle of Saratoga, you can bet that term paper wasn't about military tactics.

## Massachusetts Hall—Harvard University

### *The Student Who Never Was*

When someone finds out their house is haunted, there are a few reactions. One way to handle a haunting is just to learn to live with the spirit. The second approach, probably the most typical, is to totally freak out and call in whatever help you can find—priests, exorcists, paranormal research teams, shamans, whoever.

A third approach—confronting the ghost—was taken by an assistant dean at Harvard's famous Massachusetts Hall, the oldest still-standing building on campus. Most of the building is used as office space, although the fourth floor has rooms for freshmen. It appeared that those freshman dorms attracted another guest to Massachusetts Hall.

No one knows when Holbrook Smith started to appear, but stories of a strange visitor who would stop by and chat with the students began to circulate, eventually reaching the assistant dean. A man described as a "tall respectable-looking older gentleman" who claimed to be a member of the class of 1914 would drop by and talk with the students for the first weeks of the new term. Most of the students enjoyed the chats with the old-timer. They didn't even seem to care about the strange phenomena that occurred when Mr. Smith left. After a few meetings with Smith, the students noticed that when he left no one ever heard a door open or close.

E. Fred Yalouris, of the class of '71, describes the man. "He was in his late fifties or early sixties—this was back in '67–'68—and he was dressed in wing-tipped shoes and a tweed jacket, very Ivy. The man came into B entryway one day and knocked on our door. He proceeded to sit and talk, always very gracious and well-spoken."

Burriss Young, assistant dean at the time, said that Holbrook, "insisted that he had lived in B entry and that he had been roommates with Senator Saltonstall in the Class of 1914, but Senator Saltonstall had not lived in B entry."

Students and faculty members alike were mystified at the man's ability to appear and disappear.

Yalouris told the student newspaper, "He was an obviously eccentric old gent, and his visits were characterized by a completely unannounced sort of entry into the suite and an equally strange disappearance. One time he disappeared between the fourth and the first floor of the dorm. It was quite mysterious."

A few Massachusetts Hall residents decided to investigate Holbrook Smith. After an extensive search through student records and yearbooks, the students never found anyone named Holbrook Smith in the class of 1914.

While Holbrook's visits continued—as did his claims that he belonged to the class of 1914—some students began to complain to the assistant dean, who determined it was time to confront Smith, or whoever he was.

Dean Young found Holbrook in the B-entry section of the building one day and asked him to leave.

As he looked at him, Young said that Holbrook's eyes became "the saddest eyes I've even seen."

After a few seconds, Holbrook replied, "You've ruined a perfectly good thing."

Holbrook turned around and walked away. He was never seen again.

At least that's what the administration thought.

The ghost of Holbrook Smith may not have totally disappeared from Massachusetts Hall. Students invoke his name when weird events occur in Massachusetts Hall. For example, the ghost of Holbrook Smith is blamed when authorities discover a stash of liquor hidden in a student's room.

Mass Hall has other spirits. The same assistant dean said that students have encountered other phantoms in the building. It seems to be natural to encounter the unnatural in Harvard's oldest structure.

As Dean Young said, "Eighteenth-century buildings should have ghosts. If there are going to be ghosts, it makes sense they should live in the nicest building in the Yard."

# Ecology House—Cornell University

*Ghost Tales Grow from Tragedy at Ecology House*

The students who live in Ecology House, better known as the friendly Eco House and occasionally the Hurlburt House, are some of Cornell's seriously fun students. They manage to mix the weighty topics of global climate change and ecological well-being with the zany and lighthearted, like their Dr. Seuss theater troupe and Eco Hoe Downs.

Visitors say that a warm, communal spirit emanates from the building full of student do-gooders. It's easy to forget that the property was once the site of Cornell's deadliest tragedies. But, other spirits that emanate from the Ecology House would never let us forget the tragedy the occurred April 5, 1967. During the early morning hours of April 5, a fire tore through the Eco House, which was then called the Cornell Heights Residential Club.

The 62 survivors describe the hellish blaze as a wall of flames and a seemingly impassable wall of black smoke. Some students jumped out. Others fashioned ropes made of sheets.

Eight students and one professor were not so lucky; they died in the blaze.

Cornell faculty, staff, and student body were devastated. A memorial service drew more than 1,200 people from the Cornell community, thousands more listened to the service that was broadcast over the university's loudspeaker system.

The reading was from Lysicdas, a poem by Milton, that contains the line, "For Lycidas is dead, dead ere his prime."

The bells tolled for the victims, the solemn tones echoed over the silent, somber campus.

Ever since the tragedy, restless spirits have made their presence known at the refurbished Residential Club. The activity has ranged from physical and strange electromagnetic phenomena to actual apparitions. Witnesses report seeing strange lights and hearing voices, even when no one else is present. Footsteps slap down the hall. There have even been reports of a ghost dog barking in the building. The dog, or so the story goes, was another victim of the blaze.

Residents don't seem bothered by the supernatural. They're just reminders of the tragedy.

And, maybe, they say, it's important to remember those who were dead, dead ere their prime.

## Risley Hall—Cornell University

*Auntie Pru? Where Are You?*

Risley Hall, named after Prudence Risley, is a residence hall for the school's performing artists.

Impromptu Frisbee matches and football games break out on the lawns of other Cornell residence halls. Not at Risley. They stage dramatic, swashbuckling sword fights on the Risley Hall lawn.

All under the watchful eye of Auntie Pru.

Auntie Pru is the ghost of Prudence Risley and the spirit behind some of the inexplicable events that occur in Risley.

For example, students say they hear noises that don't have a source. They also notice the lights flickering on and off. Again, there doesn't seem to be a reason for the electrical disturbances.

One thing witnesses agree on—you know Auntie Pru is in your presence when you feel the cool draft that accompanies her entrance to the world of the living. Temperature shifts are, after all, well known in the field of parapsychology as evidence of ghostly presences.

Why does Auntie Pru appear in Cornell?

Students think she's just keeping watch on them. There may be another explanation. Risley Hall is full of creative, passionate artists, just the type of people who would be open to paranormal experiences.

## Maricopa Residence Hall—University of Arizona
*Campus Legend of Suicide Victim Haunts This Residence Hall*

Maricopa Residence Hall is the spot of the University of Arizona's favorite spooky story. It's also a story that evenly divides the paranormal community and student body of the university.

The story goes like this:

Once there was a female student who went to the University of Arizona back in the turn of the century. (In some versions, she's the daughter of the university's president, but we'll just go with the generic rendition.)

She lived in the Maricopa Residence Hall, the oldest residence hall on campus.

The student soon fell in love with a fellow student. That happens all the time, right? And, normally, everyone's happy when a classmate hooks up. But, among her friends at the school, the beau's reputation wasn't exactly sterling. He was rumored to be a bit of a playboy. But, as is often the case, love is blind—and a little hard of hearing. The student shut out her friends' protests when she announced that she was going to be engaged.

It wasn't too long after the engagement that the student stumbled on her fiance locked in an embrace with another woman.

Distraught, she ran back to the Maricopa, where she fastened a noose made from rope, tied it to the ceiling, and hanged herself. Where the incident happened is a matter of conjecture. Reports have placed the scene of the suicide in the third floor, second floor, and even in the building's creepy, old basement. (The basement has my vote.)

Ever since then, the Maricopa has been haunted by the ghost of a lovelorn girl, who appears to be sobbing. Strange noises also emanate from the basement, according to the legend.

Here's where the debate comes in.

It's a good story, but have there been any confirmed sightings of the ghost or any evidence of her presence? Have there been one or two firsthand reports? In other words, is the jilted Maricopa ghost just a campus legend?

One student told a reporter that while she didn't see the ghost, her friend did.

"But I think she was drunk," the student added.

## Freeman Hall—Iowa State University
### *Iowa State Halls Have Harrowing Tales*

Legends of ghosts stalking dormitories are nothing new in haunted higher education. They come from a lot of sources, and are tales told and cherished by alumni and current students. When the source of a paranormal encounter is a law-enforcement official, however, the chances increase that the force involved isn't just a viral story passed on from class to class; it's an honest-to-goodness ghostly encounter.

A ghostly encounter is exactly what happened to one Iowa State security official during Thanksgiving break several years ago. The campus was deserted—just as it was supposed to be at Thanksgiving. That wasn't the problem. The problem was a face staring out of the window of Freeman Hall. The security official said he noticed it right away.

No one was supposed to be in the building.

The investigative intuition of the officer went into overdrive. The figure in Freeman Hall could be a vandal or prowler who found the opportunity for mayhem at a deserted residence hall too tempting to skip. After using his radio to report the suspected break-in to security headquarters, the officer went in. He stalked through the dark dorm, walked upstairs, and moved toward the spot where he saw the face.

Or thought he saw the face.

There was no one in the dorm.

We could chalk this incident up to mistaken identity or simply an overzealous security officer, but other witnesses have had run-ins with the mysterious face. A Freeman Hall residence administrator said she was walking back along the deserted path that led to Freeman Hall. Thanksgiving break had just started and, like the security officer, the RA figured that most of the students were gone. That's why she was startled when her eyes seemed to be drawn toward the upper floors of the dorm she watched over.

Staring back at the RA were the vacant eyes of a woman. The woman then stepped away from the window, turned, and vanished. The RA was dumbfounded. Who would stay behind during the break? She went to investigate, but like the security officer who scoured the empty dorm for a figure that did not exist, the RA discovered that the dorm was, indeed, empty. While she never discovered who the solitary figure looking at her from Freeman Hall was, she stumbled onto something even more disturbing.

The RA remembered that the woman—or whatever was looking at her from the window—turned and walked away. Except, if a flesh and blood human would have walked in that direction, she wouldn't have gone very far—there was a solid wall in the path.

There was only one explanation—the RA had just made eye contact with the ghost of Freeman Hall.

The ghost that the security officer and the RA saw is a matter of conjecture, but the safe bet is that it's the spirit of Alice Freeman Palmer, a pioneering female educator. The story is that Alice thirsted to pursue an education at a time when it wasn't exactly encouraged to do so. She had to take teaching jobs and tutoring gigs to pay her way through college.

It sounds like Alice never forgot how tough it was to go to school. Her spirit continues to help the students in her namesake hall.

The ghost of Alice Freeman Palmer performs some chores for the students so hopefully they have more time for class and study. One resident said that she came home from class one day and thanked her roommate for making her bed. She remembered it wasn't made when she left the dorm that morning. But her roommate said she didn't make her bed—and her roommate said her bed was made, too.

In another incident, a Freeman resident was shocked when her stereo turned on by itself and, later, the television began to flip through channels all by itself—the remote, the resident said—was nowhere near her at the time. Alice, no doubt, was trying to find something educational on the TV.

These examples of strange phenomena join a list of other weird happenings experienced by residents, including slamming doors and flickering lights.

Alice Freeman Palmer, though, isn't the only ghost who haunts her namesake dormitory. The famous nurse, Clara Barton, makes an appearance in Iowa State University lore.

## Barton Hall—Iowa State University
### *Death Stalks Clara Barton*

Right next to Freeman Hall is another haunted dorm—Barton Hall.

The building is named for one of America's great pioneers not just in the medical field, but also a pioneer in the push for equal rights for women. As founder of the Red Cross, Clara Barton rescued the injured from battlefields, dared to care for those sick with influenza, and made a case that women deserved to work and serve wherever men do.

According to those who have stayed in Iowa State's Barton Hall, the spirit of Clara Barton still has an attachment for the residence hall that bears her name and for the students who live within.

According to one freshman who was staying on Barton Hall's third floor, Clara is still checking on her patients. Her ghost made an unexpected check of her floor.

Angela Jones told the student newspaper that she was fast asleep one night, when she awoke to hear someone walking down the halls.

The rhythm and echo of the footfalls were unmistakable. The sound wasn't just some random building noise.

Jones said it couldn't have had a human origin either. It was late, and there was no one awake in the dorm.

The incident backed up a story that her friend told her earlier. Her friend said that one night in the summer when Barton Hall was locked, she looked at the dorm and could see that the upper floor was "glowing." Was this glowing spirit just Clara walking down the third-floor hall?

Like Alice Freeman Palmer, who appears in Freeman Hall, Clara has a good reputation among the students for being a beneficial spirit.

"But Barton is a good ghost," Jones said. "She looks over you. She doesn't haunt you. She's a friendly ghost."

## Linden Hall—Iowa State University

*Paranormal Light Show at Linden*

Residents of Linden Hall, another one of Iowa State's haunted dorms, say they've experience fantastic light shows—and they're not the result of listening to too much Pink Floyd music while indulging in a little too much of the university's social life.

The light shows at Linden Hall are of the paranormal sort.

One student, Lindsay Rathe, a sophomore at the time, said she woke up in her Linden Hall room at 3 a.m., which is, according to many paranormal researchers, a particularly haunted time. While she was still groggy, she noticed that her desk was "glowing." Interestingly, she claimed it was glowing with an "invisible" light. That's a pretty apt description of phantom lights—lighting effects caused by spirits.

Rathe thought—or maybe, hoped—that she was dreaming. But, as the fear began to bubble up inside her, she realized it wasn't a dream; she was yet another victim of the Linden Hall haunting.

She requested to be moved from the haunted second floor to the less paranormally active third floor.

Over the years, students who lived in sections of Linden Hall claimed the dorm "just wasn't right." Certain sections had a particularly creepy feeling about them, too. Stories of apparitions and inexplicable occurrences continue to be passed around Linden Hall and around campus.

Kyle Regan, another sophomore resident of the haunted dorm, said he was in the bathroom when the water faucet turned on. "This wasn't just a trickle," Regan said, "something that could easily be blamed on a bad washer or a faulty pipe. The faucet was gushing out at full blast."

Regan did what any sane person would do: he shut the water off and ran out of the bathroom. I wouldn't have even turned the faucet off—conservation be damned.

There was more haunting in store for the freshman. Regan and other residents watched on a few occasions as a screen door would open and close, even though there were no breezes or wind gusts.

Mirrors, which can be spiritual portals, are vulnerable to the dorm's paranormal energies. Students have said they don't just see their reflections in the mirror; they see the images of ghosts!

Still other witnesses have seen ghosts of football players on Saturday. Of course, Saturdays are big game days for college football players. The sighting of the gridiron ghost adds evidence to those who believe the most popular legend of Linden Hall's haunting. Some students believe that a football player committed suicide in the building. Since then, his restless spirit haunts the halls of his former dorm room.

You might say it's his eternal penalty.

## Perkins Hall—Ohio University

### *The Dorm of Distrubances*

Perkins Hall isn't typically mentioned as one of the haunted spots on the Ohio University campus. And that's what ticks off a lot of former and current residents of Perkins. The residence hall, they claim, has some of the most believable and confirmed accounts of paranormal activity, enough to place the dorm right there with the Ridges and Wilson Hall on the list of the university's most haunted.

A series of stories told by a former Perkins Hall RA to ForgottenOhio.com offers the best evidence. She claimed to have had several run-ins with an unseen presence while at Perkins, as well as heard stories from other residents.

In one incident, the student was alone in the building two weeks before the residents were slated to move in. While the rest of the staff was at a nearby dorm watching a movie, this student was busy hanging a television cable. As she stood on a chair, she heard a voice distinctly say, "Hey!"

The voice sounded like it was coming from the hall, but the RA could plainly see that the hall was empty.

The incident frightened the student so much, she climbed off the chair and made a quick call to the dorm where her staff was enjoying the movie. She thought maybe someone came back early from the movie, but, to her confusion, everyone was accounted for. No one left. She was still alone. Or at least that's what she thought.

Throughout the semester, the paranormal activity continued.

Once, while hanging Halloween decorations for a contest, the RA said she led a few other girls to her room to show them some decorations. As the RA walked to her bed on the far side of the room, the girls heard a bone-chilling laugh. The girls screamed and ran from the room. A few moments later, when another Perkins Hall resident went to her room to retrieve some tape, the stereo turned on all by itself.

The RA also said that her own television turned on by itself and, on a few occasions, the dorm fridge would open on its own.

Other visitors to the RA's haunted dorm had their own terrifying experience. One visitor said that when the RA temporarily left the room, a strange presence filled the room. She felt like something menacing was standing in front of her. Whatever this presence was, it wasn't happy. In fact, it was "confrontational."

The feeling that something supernatural had entered the room was followed by real physical phenomena. The student watched as the blades of the fan began to spin, slowly at first, but eventually building speed. Since it was winter, all the windows were closed, so the blades were not catching a stray breeze from outside.

When the room temperature appeared to plummet, the guest had enough. She went screaming to find the RA and told her what she experienced. She never went back into the RA's room, unless she was escorted.

She became yet another unsuspecting supporter for Perkin's inclusion on the list of best haunts of Ohio University.

# More Ohio University Haunts

## *An Assortment of Spirits and Supernatural Events at the Scariest Place on Earth*

In most universities, students are eager to find out which buildings are haunted on campus; at Ohio University, the students find it easier just to find out which buildings aren't haunted.

Nearly every dorm, classroom, and administrative building has a supernatural tale or two attached to it. They're not always the most documented, or most investigated, but the supernatural activity is worth reviewing. Here are some other haunted hot spots at Ohio University.

### WASHINGTON HALL

At Washington Hall, the campus's reputation for spooky activity hits its most grandiose. Not content with one or two ghosts, Washington Hall is reportedly haunted by an entire basketball team.

One dorm resident said she heard the squeaking of sneakers when the place was deserted. Another time, she woke up at night and felt chills. She also said she sensed there was a spirit near her.

## JEFFERSON HALL

Not far from Washington is one of Ohio University's other haunted dorms, Jefferson Hall. Named after the country's third president, Jefferson was built in 1956. Jefferson Hall, by most accounts, gets its haunted reputation from an incident that happened in 1996.

In 1996, a group of residents who were perplexed by a series of strange events and sightings staged a ghost hunt. The group made it to the attic without incident, but once they entered the attic room, they saw an older lady who appeared to be dressed in 1950s-era clothes. She looked like a schoolteacher.

The team was a little shocked when they saw her, but the surprises were just beginning. As they looked down, they noticed that the apparition's feet were not touching the ground. She was floating!

Making a quick exit, the courage-challenged ghost hunters sought help with the RA. The RA accompanied the team back to the spot of the full-body apparition only to discover that the doors to the room were securely locked.

Additional stories began to roll in, pun intended. Besides the occasional flashing lights, some students reported that the toilet paper rolls unrolled all by themselves.

# Bruce Hall—University of Pittsburgh

### *The Haunting of Harriet*

Pitt students—most of whom are away from home and family for the first time—quickly latch on to their dorm as a new home and their dormmates as new family.

They're also the psychic center of some of Pitt's most famous hauntings.

Bruce Hall leads the way in nonliving residence life at Pitt. The dorm is considered one of the most haunted spots on campus.

The reputation is not lost on the people who work there. Most take tales of poltergeist activity and wandering spirits in stride, determining to live with the spirit in harmony. One of the staff's holiday traditions is to hang out a stocking for each of the dorm's employees. They even make sure that there's a stocking for Harriet. Although she shows up quite regularly, Harriet isn't really a Pitt employee. In fact, she's not even really alive.

Harriet is the name that students and staff have given to the ghost who supposedly haunts the mysterious Bruce Hall.

Bruce Hall is named after former chancellor Robert Bruce, who is regarded as the first chancellor of Pitt, even though it was named Western University of Pennsylvania at the time.

One of Bruce's famous students included Thomas Mellon, who founded the Mellon financial empire. Mellon remembered Chancellor Bruce fondly in his autobiography:

"He was highly cultured in general literature, an extensive reader, liberal minded, and a most accurate scholar in the several branches he professed. He had all the philosophy of Bacon and Descartes, Hume, Reid, and Dugald Stewart at command—he had himself been a student of Dugald Stewart."

Bruce Hall, on Fifth Avenue, is part of the Schenley Quad, a section of the Pitt campus that holds up to eight residence halls, and was once called the Schenley Apartments. And, of course, the Schenley name has been associated with several other Pitt hauntings, including the ghosts that stalk the university's soaring Cathedral of Learning.

Even though the staff and students of Bruce Hall dubbed the ghost Harriet, there's still a bit of confusion as to who is really behind the hauntings. We can't be sure if the ghost is male or female. Or that it's even a ghost, or a poltergeist.

Whatever the origin, one story about the Bruce Hall haunting goes like this:

When it was an apartment building, the owner or caretaker (the reports vary) lived on the twelfth floor. For several years, he had been involved in an affair, at least that's one version of the story.

One of the people involved in this love triangle committed suicide. The story varies here, too. In some reports, the wife committed suicide; in others, the mistress takes her own life. There are even other stories that indicate that the husband, upset by the shame he brought on his family, kills himself. Most reports say that the suicide occurred in the stairwell.

The tales of the love-triangle-gone-bad do agree on one thing: a spirit has unfinished business in Bruce Hall.

No one knows exactly when the spirit encounters started in Bruce Hall, but the stories of something amiss in the building were circulated before it became a dorm. So we can't just blame the exuberance of college kids for the stories.

A few Schenley Apartment dwellers say they saw a spirit wandering in the stairwell. Tales of paranormal events filtered out, too. Residents would come home and find tables and chairs moved, even though apartment rooms were locked tight. Renters blamed the managers, or employees, for sneaking into rooms, even as management protested that they—or their workers—had nothing to do with the sudden redecoration efforts in the apartments.

No one knows whether the university knew they were buying haunted goods when they turned the apartment building into residence halls. But the stories didn't disappear when the lease was signed.

In fact, the tales of something mysterious and spooky haunting Bruce Hall grew at a torrid pace when Pitt assumed ownership.

Bruce Hall's Banquet Hall is a prime haunting location.

You may, after this story, be able to detect a theme among Pitt haunts. The ghosts at Pitt are foodies. Like the spirit, or spirits, who haunt the Cathedral of Learning, a few spooks like to visit the banquet room in Bruce Hall. Over the years, workers have claimed to witness a series of strange events that convinced them that a spirit was present.

One report centers on the doors of the storage cabinets. People say these doors inexplicably open and close. At other times, the cabinets just rattle. One witness said that each time the workers left the room, they heard a sharp "bang" of a cabinet door. When the workers returned, the room was eerily still and silent. Despite the stillness and no sign of human intervention, the now freaked-out banquet workers say they still felt a presence was watching over them.

Could it be that Harriet was an unhappy banquet manager during her former life? The ghost seems to be particularly concerned about table settings, much to the frustration of the staff's current banquet organizers.

If the table isn't set just so, Harriet apparently tosses napkins on the floor, workers say. Skeptics easily dismiss this manifestation as a practical joker on the staff, or blame it on a random wind gust, but workers say those explanations can't explain away the strange activity. They point out that other napkins aren't disturbed, even though they are in the direct path of the phantom breeze, and no one has ever admitted to pulling a prank.

Banquet workers at Pitt are meticulous about their work. One might say they're so meticulous at making everything look so perfect that they could use some counseling. Maybe Harriet knows the staff's little compulsive tendencies and, just to get on their nerves, she jumbles up the place settings. Workers say they've discovered spoons and forks moved around.

Harriet, or whoever the ghost of the banquet hall is, may or may not be the same spook roaming Bruce Hall's twelfth floor. If it is the same, Harriet's behavior in other parts of Bruce Hall is much more intense. Students have reported sounds in the stairwell, like someone walking—or running—up and down the steps. The same sound of frantic footwork echoes through the twelfth floor. But, when witnesses peek around the corner to see who's making the racket, there's nobody there.

Some witnesses also report hearing a voice—a woman's voice—echoing in the same stairwell.

Could these be the spirit reminders of the tragic love triangle, as some students speculate?

The elevator is another hot spot for paranormal activity in the building, witnesses say. More than one unsuspecting rider has jumped on the elevator and ended up taking a ride into the twilight zone. They report that, despite the buttons they push, the elevator automatically deposits them on Bruce Hall's haunted twelfth floor. One visitor said the elevator stopped at the twelfth floor and then refused to budge—either up or down—until she wisely made a break for it. She jumped out of the elevator and headed to the stairwell. Unfortunately, she soon found out that the twelfth floor stairwell is haunted, too. As she walked down the steps, she heard those famous footsteps. At first, she thought the sounds were nothing more than an echo of her own footsteps. So, she stopped.

And the sound of footsteps kept coming. Closer. The sounds echoed out a few flights above her.

She immediately picked up the pace and ran to the exit.

After this escape from Bruce Hall's cursed elevator, she made a quick exit from the building and entered into Bruce Hall's haunted history.

## Halcyon House—Georgetown University

### *Did Spirits Force Georgetown to Sell a Famous Home?*

By all accounts, Georgetown University was both proud—and lucky—that the stunning and historic Halcyon House had fallen into its hands in the 1960s. Besides being one of the toniest properties in the Washington, D.C., area, its enormous interior fit the space needs of a growing university. It would be the perfect dorm for the first official class of female Hoyas.

But Halcyon House didn't stay as part of Georgetown very long. It was sold a few short years later and the university began building Darnall and Harbin Halls.

Why did the university unload the Georgian mansion so quickly? Was the official reason—zoning restrictions—the actual reason for the quick sale? Or, was there another explanation—a supernatural explanation—that the school officials unloaded the would-be female dorm.

Those who say that the university experienced paranormal real estate cold feet say that the answer lies in the history of Halcyon House— and its extensive haunted reputation as one of D.C.'s most paranormal properties.

The land that Halcyon sits on was once owned by Charles Calvert, Third Lord of Baltimore. In the early 1700s, he gave several hundred acres of the land, which would one day be a large chunk of Washington, D.C., to a man named Ninian Beall. Beall was known for his zealous belief in Presbyterianism. Some say the origins of the haunting started with Beall. But Beall was just one of many owners who could serve as possible sources of the paranormal activity.

In fact, the home had a whole slew of owners with big personalities. And when it comes to hauntings, big personalities leave behind lots of residual psychic energy One of the owners was Albert Clemens. If the last name sounds familiar, Albert was the nephew of Samuel Clemens, better known as Mark Twain.

Albert may have left his psychic mark on Halcyon House.

In some cases of paranormal activity, it's not the people, but the purpose that creates a haunting. Besides being centered in a city that withstood battles, assassinations, and all manner of political intrigue, Halcyon House reportedly served as a station on the Underground Railroad, a safe house for slaves escaping to the north. This piece of history also mixes in with the building's haunted tableau.

One of the first ghosts said to haunt Halcyon is the spirit of a wounded British soldier. The soldier may be a remnant of the Revolutionary War, or he could be a soldier from the band of Brits who invaded the nation's young capital during the War of 1812. His spirit, though, has been seen and even heard by more than a few inhabitants and guests of the mansion.

Once, a carpenter working at the house heard moans and cries coming from the basement. But he knew that no one else was in the building. There are some people who love to investigate the unknown. Not this guy. The carpenter left the home in such a hurry that he forgot his tools. And he never came back for them, either. The cries may have been psychic reminders of the soldier's spirit. Or, as some other investigators have speculated, these moans are sonic reminders of escaped slaves who might have hid in the building's basement.

The 1960s was an extremely haunted era for Halcyon House.

According to one couple who rented an apartment in the building, they were shocked when they saw a bald, chubby man in a brown suit sitting in one of their chairs. He was no friend of theirs. He wasn't a guest—at least a corporeal guest. They had no idea who the man in the brown suit was.

But when they saw a picture of Albert Clemens, they were sure Mark Twain's nephew was their unexpected visitor.

Another resident who lived in Halcyon House for about six years had a female visitor. This resident claimed he saw the spirit of an old woman in his bedroom. But, unlike Albert Clemens, who would probably be classified as a residual spirit—a manifestation that doesn't necessarily interact with the world of the living—this spirit was decidedly interactive. The resident claimed that the spirit would rearrange the covers on his bed every night.

But, one night, the spirit did something profoundly unexpected. She reached up to the resident, kissed him, and promised never to bother him again. With that pronouncement, the woman eerily glided out the window.

She might have glided back, though.

Years later, a husband and wife, who were Georgetown faculty members, were hosting a cocktail party. A guest drifted away from the gathering and went upstairs.

When she came back, she asked the husband how long his mother had been living with them.

The professor was surprised.

"My mother's been dead for several years," he explained to the guest.

The guest looked a little ill.

"Then who is the woman rocking in the chair upstairs?" she asked.

The couple didn't have a good answer, but they chalked it up to the numerous spirits that called Halcyon House their home.

You can't find many documented cases of hauntings during the period that Georgetown University used the Halcyon House. But there's this strange bit of circumstantial evidence.

There's an old real estate legend that if you see a house on your block that's sold, then sold soon after, and then sold again soon after that, there's one reason: it's haunted. Some have speculated that Georgetown dumped Halcyon for the same reason.

## Room 4714—West Point

*Unlocking West Point's Forbidden Barracks*

You know that when an outbreak of paranormal activity appears in *Time* magazine that you have hit a whole other level of campus ghost stories. In the 1970s, the magazine reported on one of the Military Academy's most famous paranormal run-ins; the incident started around Halloween in the 47th Division barracks.

Two plebes—West Point-ese for freshman—were stationed in Room 4714. It was a typical room by West Point's spartan standards. The room is equipped with the bare minimum of essentials to get a cadet through the academy's rigorous academic and military training.

But Room 4714 was equipped with a spirit.

During the night, one cadet awoke to confront the filmy presence of a soldier dressed in the ornate uniform. He carried a musket and topped off the uniform with a tall military cap—or shako. The spirit appeared to pop right out of the wall.

The cadet was not about to make this sighting public knowledge. First, he had the cool-steel resolve of most cadets. And, he wasn't about to taint the reputation of the academy with a bizarre tale of supernatural activity. Instead, he entrusted the information with his friend and roommate. Both did what any good soldier would do to an invader; they laid an ambush for the ghost.

Sure enough, as the cadets waited, the ghost appeared again. The ghost popped out of the wall, stood for awhile, and then receded back into the wall.

The roommate was able to confirm the sighting. The cadets began to tell their story. First, they told their friends. Word spread from there until it finally reached Cadet Captain Keith Bakken. Captain Bakken and an upperclassman decided to put an end to the haunted rumors. They, too, staked out the room.

Captain Bakken said the spirit appeared to them, too. (He's still a believer, according to the magazine account.)

News then spread quickly, as did possible explanations.

The U.S. Naval Academy, erstwhile athletic rivals of Army, said that the appearance was a clever prank pulled by a few Naval Academy midshipmen. They claim they sneaked into West Point and planted a projector that would flash the image on the room's walls.

Cadets think this is just misinformation by their erstwhile foes. As proof, believers add that an informal paranormal investigation was held in the room. The investigators noted some serious swings in temperature.

The roommate's account—that the spirit appeared to "pop" out of the walls—also seems to contradict the midshipmen's explanation that the ghost was a mere projection of a two-dimensional photograph on the wall.

And then there's the reaction of the academy's administration. Room 4714 was closed forever. That's one way to take care of ghost stories.

If a haunting is enough for West Point administrators to close off a room, they may consider closing the basement of Thayer House.

## Thayer House—West Point

*A Brigade of Ghosts Haunt Thayer*

If there was any one man who could be credited with establishing the military academy as a great learning institution for soldiers, it's Colonel Syvanous Thayer.

Thayer House, a majestic federal-style house on the West Point campus, is reportedly the most haunted spot at the military academy. Witnesses believe that there isn't just one ghost at Thayer; there are several. There are so many that America's most famous ghost hunters were called in for a covert op.

Ed and Lorraine Warren, who were pioneers in ghost hunting, had not heard the stories about the superintendent's mansion at West Point before they entered the home.

One story was that an Irish cook named Molly haunted Thayer. Other witnesses said they saw the ghost of a man, presumed to be a former superintendent, stalking through the halls.

Nor did the couple know that they weren't the first ghost hunters sent in to battle the spirits of Thayer. A priest had been called in during the 1920s. Two young servant girls were scared by a spirit—and sent running, naked, into the cold New York night.

In fact, Ed and Lorraine thought they had been called just to give a talk about the spiritual subjects when they arrived on the grounds of West Point in October 1972.

But, the day before the lecture, an executive officer at West Point asked for the couple to engage in a security mission after the talk. Lorraine said the officer was vague, but said he would send a car for the couple.

After a mysterious black limousine dropped them off at the academy, the ghost hunters were greeted by the executive officer. The officer, a major, engaged in some good-natured chitchat. Then, he got down to business. The major said that there was a security breech at Thayer House and he inquired if Ed and Lorraine would help.

They agreed, but had to be wondering how a demonologist and his clairvoyant wife could help the military with a security problem.

The major, however, quickly added, "Between us ... there's a ghost in the general's quarters."

The general, the major said, was interested in getting to the bottom of the haunting and to determine, once and for all, whether the cause of the strange activity in Thayer House was natural—or not.

An Army photographer and other staff who would help collect information accompanied the couple as they swept through the house. Ed and Lorraine were told all the material collected would be government property. In other words, this was a top-secret mission.

The general and his wife met Ed and Lorraine at Thayer House. The general, who Lorraine said seemed nice and wise, filled them in on the phenomena. He told them about the office in the building's basement. The office is securely locked up. However, no matter how securely the room is locked, and no matter how neatly the office bunk is made, when they reenter the office, the bunk is discovered completely messed up.

The general added that ghosts have been reported upstairs, although admitted never seeing them.

Another issue—personal items were temporarily missing. Ed and Lorraine noted the general was careful not to say, "stolen," because the items would end up reappearing. That was clearly a human spirit at work, Ed told the general.

This activity seemed to bother the general the most. Guests who have attended some functions at Thayer reported that they had items stolen, and their pockets picked. It was quite embarrassing.

Ed, Lorraine, the general, his wife, and the rest of the staff started their hunt at the basement office. The bunk, as usual, was torn apart. The general also pointed out that a wet spot on the cutting board in the kitchen would nearly dry—and then reappear the next day.

As they continued their tour, Lorraine would stop and close her eyes. She waited for psychic impressions, but so far there were none. It wasn't until the group entered the back bedroom when Lorraine saw a spirit—the spirit of John F. Kennedy.

Lorraine was almost afraid to say what she saw, but she noticed the astounded look on the general's face. It turns out, as the general explained, the back bedroom was President Kennedy's room. The president's bad back made climbing the stairs difficult, so he stayed on the ground-level room.

But Lorraine had more startling revelations. She picked up impressions of several spirits. Almost every room was haunted!

In an upstairs bedroom, Lorraine detected the presence of a strong woman. The general knew right away who it was: General Douglas MacArthur's mother had lived in the room.

Despite Lorraine's stunning ability to detect spirits in the house, the general and his staff were slightly disappointed. The spirits just didn't seem to be behind the aggressive disturbances in Thayer. Lorraine suggested she return after the lecture to try to make contact with the spirit through a trance.

The group reconvened for the trance session.

Lorraine did make contact with the spirit of a black man who was accused of murder in the basement of Thayer. The spirit told Lorraine that despite being exonerated by the Army, the man felt that his name was dishonored.

The psychic communicated to the spirit that there was no dishonor. At that, the spirit faded away. Unfortunately, the general told Lorraine that the trance results were likely a miss. To his knowledge, there was no black man who stayed in Thayer. Still, he told the ghost hunters that he would check the records.

Weeks later, the general called Lorraine. As it turned out, a black man—who served as a porter—was accused of a murder at Thayer. And that he was later exonerated by the Army!

The general was amazed.

Reports are that Thayer continues to be haunted. It's hard to tell whether the porter continues to express his anger at the false accusation. After all, there isn't a shortage of spirits at haunted Thayer.

# 3.

# CLASSROOMS AND ADMINISTRATIVE BUILDINGS

Researchers who study paranormal phenomena point to at least one thread that seems to tie the world of the undead with the world of the living: energy.

They suggest that since energy is never created or destroyed, it can be converted to a kind of psychic residue that remains in places long after a person has passed on. This is one way that paranormal activity is explained. High-intensity events and highly emotional people leave their psychic imprints on an environment.

The folks at the university Physics Department probably have a few qualms with the idea, but the theory fits nicely with why universities seem so haunted.

If you have ever visited a university around finals, the nervous energy is palpable. Or, try to embed yourself in the student section during a sporting event. It's easy to imagine that this seething, raucous energy could be etched into the very reality around it.

The psychic energy–conversion theory is one reason that buildings with classrooms seem to be the most haunted campus structures. They are often the settings for high-emotion events, whether it's the anxiety about an upcoming test, the thought of a romantic encounter, or the desperation of a homesick student.

Famous professors and students can also attach themselves to classrooms, according to researchers who, as proof, can offer dozens of accounts of apparitions that appear to resemble former teachers and students.

Administrative buildings, which serve as headquarters for the university or various departments, join classroom buildings as some of the most haunted spots on campus. While heightened psychic energy is usually blamed for the paranormal activity in classrooms, administrative buildings tend to attract more residual forms of spirits. Residual ghosts are spiritual energies left over from previous lives. Like an embedded music or video file, this energy continually repeats the same act—or sound, or even smell—over and over again. Witnesses may catch a glimpse of a famous university president walking down the hall. They may see a group of deans meeting in the lobby. These are residual spirits.

The English Building at the University of Illinois is a good place to start on our investigation into haunted classrooms and university administrative buildings.

This imposing structure has it all: poltergeists, residuals, and interactive spirits. For good measure, students have thrown in some urban legends to enhance the mystery.

# English Building—University of Illinois

*Haunt Is a Noun ... and a Verb*

The English Building, located on the west side of the University of Illinois' haunted Quad, is considered one of the university's most paranormal places on campus. You get that otherworldly impression when you first see the building's impressive façade.

It wouldn't take much for one of the university's talented fiction writers to dream up a story about a ghost or two haunting the English Building. In fact, those stories have been spread by students and alumni for decades—and now the tales are making their way around the world on the Internet.

According to one version of the oft-told tale, the explanation of the English Building's haunted origins goes like this: The building, which used to be a girl's dormitory, is haunted by a spirit known as "Christie"— a supposed murder victim. Her story is tinged with details that make it sound more like an urban legend than a factual account of a murder. But, sometimes, as any good English student will tell you, reality is stranger than fiction.

Christie roomed on the top floor of the building. One night, Christie's roommate went out, while Christie stayed in. Her roommate decided she would stay overnight in a room a few stories below. Later that night, she went back to her top-floor room to get a pillow and a few things. The room was pitch black. And silent. After whispering the name, "Christie," a few times to rouse her roommate, she decided that since Christie was obviously asleep, she wouldn't turn on the lights. She struggled through the dark to find her bed and grabbed the pillow and exited as quietly as she could.

The next morning she went back to her room and was horrified to discover the lifeless body of Christie. She had been stabbed several times.

A message, scrawled in blood, was written on the mirror. It read: *Aren't You Glad You Didn't Turn on The Lights?*

According to the legend, the murderer was never found. At this point in the story, particularly mean storytellers would add, "and the murderer could still be out there stalking his next victim."

But, I would never do that.

Is there any evidence that a murder ever took place in the English Building? No. No police records or newspaper articles corroborate the story.

But stories like this seem to ignite the imagination—and maybe even paranormal activity.

Since the tales of the murder have been making their rounds on campus, students and staff have reported a host of strange activities. Furniture is moved. Electrical problems occur—and then, just as quickly, return to normal.

Not all students blame Christie for the rash of flickering lights, slamming doors, and other happenings at the English Building. Proponents of this theory believe the source of the paranormal phenomena isn't a murder victim; it's a suicide victim. A female student, this story speculates, committed suicide in her room, which later became a series of offices for graduate students.

Urban legend or not, several students and at least one paranormal investigative unit, believe they have had run-ins—and at least one, run-over—with the ghost of Christie, or perhaps the suicide victim.

But some students don't need any ghostbusters telling them there is a ghost. They've experienced strange activities in the building—and they have their own evidence. Ashley Klinger, a senior, told the student newspaper that she and a group of students were in the top-floor bathroom with a voice recorder. She said the team captured some unusual phenomena.

"When we reviewed it later, it sounded like (someone said), 'Get out. Get out of here.'"

Klinger also reported that the janitors in the building—people who would have the most contact with any spirit in the building—told her that strange activity happens so frequently that the workers have dubbed the ghost, "Clarabelle."

One time, while a janitor was on break, he noticed his wheeled supply cart starting to drift away. The janitor immediately called out, "Clarabelle! Stop the cart."

The cart screeched to a halt—immediately.

The lessons students learn at the University of Illinois are many. But, if you ask some of these students who have experienced the ghost of Christie, or Clarabelle, or whoever she is, they'll tell you the most valuable lesson—if you're going to pull an all-nighter, pick a study space other than the University of Illinois English Building.

## Lincoln Building—University of Illinois
### *Four Score and More Ghosts?*

Students who are chased out of the University of Illinois English Building by the wandering spirits of suicide victims and murdered coeds, might decide that the wide halls of the Lincoln Building are a supernatural-free respite where they can read and study. That would be a mistake.

The building, located just south of the English Building, was constructed in 1911.

Named after Illinois' favorite lawyer and all-round Great Emancipator, Abraham Lincoln, the building now serves as headquarters for the university's College of Liberal Arts and Sciences. It's also headquarters for an unnamed ghost that makes infrequent appearances to students, faculty, and guests.

Witnesses report the apparition has been seen more than once looking out the windows that face Wright Street. The sightings tend to occur after the building has closed, so most people don't believe it is a student of the flesh-and-blood variety.

"People on Wright Street look up and see a young girl looking down," a student told the school newspaper. "She looks sad."

Just who—or what—is behind this haunting is another campus debate.

Could it be Lincoln, himself? Or, perhaps, the lost soul of a student? Or the spirit of a faculty member who just can't let go of that cherished tenure status?

There's no end to the debate.

One of the most popular accounts is that the forlorn ghost gazing out the window is the spirit of a dead teaching assistant. The low pay, long hours, and often unglamorous work of a teaching assistant would explain the tired, lonely expression on the ghost's face.

Caroline Pahl, a freshman at the University of Illinois heard another story. She said that the tales in her sorority center on a girl who jumped out one of the windows.

Maybe the ghost of the Lincoln Building is just another campus legend. Maybe.

But as students make their way along Wright Street, most still cast a wary eye up to the window of the Lincoln Building.

With ghosts appearing at the English Building and the Lincoln Building, you might think it's fortunate that the university has a Psychology Department with a fine reputation. However ...

## Psychology Building—University of Illinois

### *Minding the Ghosts*

We continue our journey through the haunted classrooms at the University of Illinois with a stop at the eight-story Psychology Building, which houses most of the Psychology Department's research facilities. Here, faculty and students spend their days probing the mysteries of the human mind, including human learning, perception, and behavior.

And, usually at night, they are forced to probe the mysteries of parapsychology, too.

The building is another one of the university's haunted properties.

Some say the Psychology Building's haunted reputation began when a student threatened to jump from one of the building's upper-story railings. In most ghost stories, this would be the part where the student plummets to his death and lives on as a spirit that haunts the building.

That's your typical urban legend script, right?

But, according to most accounts of this event, the student never committed suicide. He walked back into the building safely.

The account indicates that the student did, however, die a few years later. His spirit, so the story goes, wandered back to the university and remains at the scene of what must have been a profound moment in this young man's tragic life. That's one theory.

But it's only one theory why the paranormal has become so normal in the halls of the Psychology Building. People encounter unexplained cold spots walking through the halls or while sitting quietly in one of the rooms. Others hear whispers—odd, unintelligible whispers. When they approach the source of these whispers, the enchanted talking is quickly silenced.

In still other cases, students hear footsteps—even though they know the building is empty.

Not everyone agrees that the building is haunted. Many faculty members say these encounters are nothing more than the working of an active imagination. Like true psychologists, they'd say, "It's all in the mind."

Those who have witnessed the spirit of the Psychology Building respond that if that's the case, it's also in the eyes, the ears, the nose, and on the raised back-of-the-neck hairs.

## Old Bryce or Kilgore House—University of Alabama
### *What Part of "Kilgore" Don't You Understand?*

As you probably know by now, strong personalities and strong emotions are integral in the creation of university hauntings.

The University of Alabama has paranormal personality-plus and a history of highly charged emotional events. But that's just the beginning.

The university seems to pull out all the stops to prompt these eerie legends, whether these accounts turn out to be just good old-fashioned student-told folklore or actual encounters with the afterlife.

For example, the cottage that sits on the site of an old insane asylum just happens to have "kill" and "gore" in its name. A spooky name and a questionable construction site are two paranormal strikes against Kilgore House, or Old Bryce, helping to make the building one of Alabama's most haunted landmarks.

Oh, did I mention the cottage is located adjacent to the university cemetery?

Strike three.

Kilgore House was originally constructed as a cottage for Charles Kilgore, the assistant steward of the Alabama Hospital for the Insane.

From most accounts, Mr. Kilgore lived a long and fruitful life at the cottage. He had a large family and even offered rooms to students who attended the nearby university. After the Kilgores moved, hospital employees continued to live in the place. Over time, though, the cottage fell into disrepair. Eventually, the university took it over and the tales of hauntings have been spreading ever since.

The paranormal community is torn between deciding who is responsible for the hauntings. There's enough blame to go around. For some, the ghosts are related to the Kilgore family. A few Kilgore kin died at a young age. Others counter that Mr. Kilgore's life wasn't any more tragic than a typical man of the age; therefore, the ghosts must be the spirits of the former inhabitants of the insane asylum.

Just as there are many possible sources for the phenomena at Kilgore House, the types of phenomena reported there are equally diverse. Apparitions and odd noises are frequently cited as proof that Kilgore is haunted.

Stories of spooky activity at Kilgore House have filtered through the student population for years, but the haunting suddenly grabbed the attention of paranormal researchers when a series of run-ins with paranormal forces made their way through the paranormal grapevine.

In September 2008, three different employees said they had strange encounters in the building. Multiple witnesses mean there was something more to it than just another college ghost story.

The phenomena ranged from strange noises to an actual apparition.

One staff member, alone in the building on Sunday, heard strange noises that sent her scurrying away from the building. Another person heard footsteps coming down the hall and then into an office. That's not too unusual, except the witness was alone and the office door was closed. Yet, the witness distinctly heard the footsteps coming from within the office!

I saved the biggie for last.

A final witness didn't just hear a ghost. She saw it. In fact, she saw the same apparition several times during the same eight-hour period.

The witness described the ghost as an African American woman in a turban, or head wrap.

A team of investigators from Tuscaloosa Paranormal Research Group were called in and immediately went to work gathering evidence. Investigators immediately encountered some activity that was hard to describe by normal means, including, "footsteps, banging, doors closing, and metal latches being thrown."

More investigators came to the site and collected dramatic EVPs (faint messages from beyond captured on a recording device) that seemed to respond directly to questions posed by the researchers.

Photographs taken during the investigation also appear to show strange mists and shadows in the building.

So, what's the verdict on the Kilgore House's paranormal potential?

The folks at Tuscaloosa Paranormal Research Group say the investigation is continuing—there are a lot of notes to compile and footage to review. However, they do offer a preliminary conclusion: "Little skepticism remains that Kilgore House is beyond the normal."

# Smith Hall—University of Alabama

*Ghosts Who Rock*

Anna Maria Della Costa, a writer for the *Tuscaloosa News*, had an up-close-and-personal brush with Crimson Tide spirits when she was assigned to write an article series about Tuscaloosa's haunted houses.

Della Costa had the pleasure—or misfortune—of tagging along with the Tuscaloosa Paranormal Research Group as they explored Smith Hall, home of the University's Department of Geological Sciences, as well as the Alabama Museum of Natural History.

The Tuscaloosa paranormal research team is the real deal, by the way. They have researched supernatural cases throughout the Tuscaloosa area and notched up more than a few investigations at the University of Alabama.

When Della Costa joined the team for an investigation, they came prepared. Armed with the latest electronic ghost detecting gizmos and gadgets, the team went to work, methodically examining each room for temperature shifts and other signs of ghostly presences, while gathering electronic voice phenomena, or EVPs. An EVP is a message—often just a whisper or groan—that isn't heard by people but can be picked up on sensitive recording equipment.

The team sat with the reporter in the conference room of Smith Hall's main floor. One of the group's cofounders, Mike Corley, recorded the EVP session as other folks talked. It seems someone else was in on the conversation, too. When the team played back Corley's recording, a "hushed" female voice whispered, quite clearly, "I love you a lot."

The reporter made it clear, no one in the group said those words.

"It wasn't me. It wasn't Liz. We were sitting too far away from the recorder," Della Costa said.

It wasn't the end of the paranormal adventures. As they exited the building, a chair on the main floor had moved. Since everyone was with the team, there was no explanation for this late-night interior design lesson.

So, who is behind the haunting of Smith Hall?

Campus legends reveal a possible culprit: Eugene Allen Smith—that's the person the building was named after. Dr. Smith was a University of Alabama professor and state geologist. You'd think a geology professor would want to stay buried, but that doesn't seem to be the case.

One of the Smith Hall legends is that Smith can be heard—of all things—driving his wagon down the halls. On some nights the building is filled with the sounds of whip cracks, horse neighs, and wagon wheel clacks. There's no explanation why Dr. Smith's wagon is being driven through the halls, but it is one way to make sure a professor makes those 8 a.m. lectures.

Other rumors persist. A boiler supposedly blew in the building, killing several students. While the story is hard to verify, a group of students claim they have proof. They heard voices echoing down the hall and thought they found the source—a classroom where the haunted boiler room was once located. When they opened the door to investigate, they found that the tables and chairs in the room were askew. Also, a lab assistant said he was pushed by an unseen entity into a closet and the door was slammed behind him. This is either the sign of a malicious supernatural entity or a fellow student who dislikes overachievers.

Another explanation should be vetted. Since the building houses the natural history museum, there could be residual energies trapped in the artifacts and exhibits. If you ever heard of haunted objects, or cursed objects, it's a similar phenomena. Energy from an object picks up the vibrations from the source, such as a human or spirit, and then releases the energy like some type of spectral instant replay.

Whatever the source of the Smith Hall haunting, Dr. Smith may not be the only ghostly professor that haunts the Crimson halls.

# Tyson Hall—University of Tennessee

*The Collegiate Version of the Haunted Mansion*

Donna Bletner, an executive director for alumni affairs at the University of Tennessee, never believed in stories of ghosts rampaging through the school. And she was certainly ready, willing, and able to shoot down haunted tales of the building she worked in, called Tyson House, a grand mansion that now serves as for the University of Tennesse's Alumni Association and the Office of Alumni Affairs.

However, even in her most skeptical moments, Bletner might admit that Tyson House looked a little haunted. With its sweeping Corinthian columns and grand porches, the mansion looks like something Edgar Allan Poe dreamed up. Or should I say nightmared up?

But Bletner didn't let appearances deceive her. She worked there for nine years without ever encountering the slightest hint of anything paranormal.

Until that one, unforgettable night.

Bletner was working late when she heard something. She knew it was late and the rest of the staff had called it a day, leaving her alone in the big mansion.

She went to investigate, leaving her room and peering down the hallway.

Nothing.

Just as she was about to laugh off her silly investigation, she heard another noise. As she slowly crept down the hall, cracks began to form in her solid wall of doubt about the supernatural.

Out of the emptiness, Bletner heard a scream.

"I went up the stairs and quickly looked for a light under all the doors," Bletner told the *Daily Beacon*, the student newspaper. "I thought that there might be someone working up there who needed my help. I didn't see anybody, so I went back downstairs and got out of there as quickly as possible."

She added, "After that, I became kind of a believer in the Tyson House ghost."

But not the only one.

Students, alumni, and faculty have told and re-told tales of haunted Tyson House since the university bought the place in 1954. Most of the stories are similar to Bletner's. Witnesses hear strange noises and get their share of shivers when in the mansion, especially when they're alone.

Not all the accounts of paranormal activity at Tyson House are merely sounds and shivers. These phenomena, while certainly real to those experiencing them, can often be attributed to natural and psychological causes. They wouldn't hold up in an argument with a hard-nosed skeptic like Bletner—at least in an argument with a skeptic like she used to be.

Another employee's tale is a little harder to explain away. Amy Williams told the paper she had just finished making preparations for a class reunion and was about to leave. She turned off the living room lights and went to the door.

Williams had a funny feeling as she prepared to exit the building. Something made her turn around.

When she did, she saw that the lights had mysteriously turned back on again!

Williams returned to the lights, clicked them off, and checked around for an explanation. With the lights off, she was still in the dark for an explanation why the lights came back on. The switch seemed to work. There didn't appear to be any wiring issues.

So she tried to make her exit—or escape—again.

One thing you learn about ghosts is they're particularly persistent. If they're not letting death push them from their houses, no living person is going to tell them to turn the lights off. This ghost wanted the lights on.

Just as Williams reached the door, she saw that the lights had turned back on.

"So I went back to turn them off a third time, and then I just left, not wanting to know if they had been turned back on again or not," she said.

Most Tennessee faithful have no trouble believing that Tyson House is haunted. There's no debate about that. But who is haunting Tyson is up for discussion. There are several suspects. One of the lead suspects is General Lawrence Tyson. General Tyson was a West Point graduate and, later, became professor of military tactics at the university. Tyson was eventually elected to the United States Senate.

Most of the renovations and expansion were completed under General Tyson's watchful eyes. It's easy to see why the never-surrender spirit of a war hero would be unlikely to give back his land and home.

Another group of believers say it's Isabella Tyson Gilpin, daughter of Lawrence and Bettie Tyson, who remains in the home.

## Career Development Center—Indiana University
### *For Hire: Ghost of Guilt-Ridden Abortionist*

At Indiana University's Bloomington campus, the Career Development Center is a hot spot for paranormal activity that, from most accounts, may one day be renamed the Supernatural Legend Development Center.

The legend of the haunting at the building begins with a doctor, tormented by how his own career developed—or, more accurately, how it failed to develop.

According to stories passed down from class to class, there was a doctor who began his practice as a normal campus medical practitioner, but he soon expanded his treatments to include a procedure that, at the time, was just as lucrative as it was illegal. At a time when Roe versus Wade sounded more like a Friday night boxing card, the doctor performed abortion surgeries for coeds who believed they had no other choice. His clients and his services, of course, were illegal and remained a secret.

But, no one could keep the acts secret from the doctor's conscience. Some people said the doctor complained that he could hear babies crying. But no one else could hear the cries.

Others said he had botched one operation and the patient died.

Wracked with grief, the legend continues, the doctor hanged himself off the stair banister. His spirit has roamed the building that is now used as the Career Development Center ever since. Students say you can't necessarily see the spirit, but you can hear strange noises. There's also a feeling that a presence is watching you.

It may not be just the tortured doctor who haunts these halls. Witnesses say that on some nights, you can hear the faint cries of babies and, if you listen even more closely, the sad lament of the doctor joins the creepy chorus.

Some employees told the student newspaper that they haven't heard the cries. But they do get a strange feeling at the center on occasion. The place just has a weird vibe.

"I haven't seen anything that is that mind-blowing," Mark Miller, Career Development Center employee, told the *Indiana Daily Student*, "but you just get this eerie unwelcoming feeling like somebody is watching you. I've definitely felt a presence."

## Old Botany Building—Penn State
### *A Ghost Walk to Remember*

Old Botany Building is situated just across East Pollock Road from Penn State's profoundly haunted Schwab Auditorium and the grave of George Atherton, a former university president.

Next to the imposing granite and stone structures that loom over the campus, Old Botany is small and quaint. Most people mistake it for a cottage. It's also the oldest academic building on campus, built in 1887.

Old Botany may be a small building, but that doesn't mean it is short on ghosts.

The ghost of Frances Atherton, the wife of George Atherton, is one suspect in the paranormal activity reported at Old Botany. Frances is often seen peering out the attic windows looking out at Schwab Theater and the grave of her husband. Some say she wears a sorrowful, almost desperate, expression, leading to speculation that she is not happy with the street—Pollock Road—that separates her from her beloved husband.

Behind Old Botany, there was once a path that stretched between magnificent spruce and pine trees. The grove is gone now, but stories of the little campus forest continue to be passed down.

On the busiest times in broad daylight, Ghost Walk, cushioned by this lush wall of trees, was quiet and serene. At night, though, many students would take alternate, and better lit, paths to get to their destinations. It's just too creepy, and the stories don't help.

In one story, Frances Atherton, wearing the same mournful expression, is seen traveling down the appropriately named, "Ghost Walk."

Frances makes it just to Pollock Road, just in sight of her husband's grave, but never crosses. What holds her back is not readily apparent from the tale.

A 1928 edition of the *Daily Collegian* indicates that the ghost isn't Frances; the apparition is that of a dead student. Legend has it that in the 1860s a ferocious blizzard hit State College, the host town of the university. Despite warnings, one student tried to trek home during the blizzard, but never made it. The student was walking on the tree-lined path that leads directly to Old Botany and froze to death. The body was discovered near where the Burrowes Building now stands on campus.

Many are convinced that people who see the filmy presence near Old Botany are actually witnessing the reenactment of that fateful winter walk when they see the shadowy figure strolling down the tree-lined Ghost Walk.

## Science Hall—University of Wisconsin
### *Where Science Meets Parascience*

Over the years, one thing has stood in the way of ghost stories and tales of hauntings—science. Those always-skeptical scientists and their rational dissection of reality have coerced students into considering concepts like ghosts and spirits as nothing more than silly superstitions. Easy for them to say; these scientists never had an office in Science Hall.

At the University of Wisconsin–Madison, students and a few open-minded professors who have spent some time in Science Hall, especially at night, say that science and all its rationality cannot convince them that the noises they heard and the random movement of objects that they have seen are nothing more than tricks of their tired, stressed minds. Leave those excuses to the Psychology Department.

It doesn't take long to figure out the source of Science Hall's paranormal activity. If any building has a right to be haunted, it's Science Hall. Let's just start at the very creation of the building—there are rumors of deaths that occurred during its construction. But that's just the foundation of this uber-spooky building. Science Hall was once home to the Anatomy Department and the study of anatomy requires lots of corpses for study and dissection.

According to UW–Madison students familiar with the legend, since elevators didn't exist at the time, the cadavers were taken to the fifth floor by a pulley and winch.

Student legend reports that dozens of corpses, body parts, and skeletons were kept in the attic of Science Hall. The long, dark, cool attic was a great place to keep these spare body parts, but, when the Anatomy Department moved, they forgot about and left behind some of the … let's call them "study aids."

Once they were rediscovered, tales of hauntings and ghostly appearances began to spread across campus.

The paranormal activity has been mostly anonymous, there's no word of ghost teachers or librarians like the ghosts who seem to haunt Wisconsin's many haunted libraries. But some witnesses swear they've seen objects move and watched as unseen hands push beakers off of shelves.

Or are these just the excuses of clumsy students?

It's all part of the Science Hall mystery, but ghosts, poltergeists, and an attic full of cadavers aren't the only mysteries lurking in Science

Hall. At one time, Science Hall was outfitted with fire escape chutes connected to Science Hall. If an experiment ever went awry, students would take a ride down to safety in the chutes.

Stories spread that these escape pods weren't fire chutes at all; they were cadaver chutes. Since there were no elevators to bring the bodies up, so the logic went, they used the chutes to dispose of the bodies.

Come to think of it, these chutes might also come in handy for the science student who encounters a ghost on Science Hall's upper floors.

Campus experts say the stories of cadaver chutes are false and, anyway, the fire chutes were dismantled during a remodeling effort at Science Hall during the 1980s.

# Morrill Hall—University of Maryland

### *More Ghosts at Morrill Hall*

Have you ever noticed a home in your neighborhood that changes hands over and over again? As soon as a family buys the home and moves in, they suddenly have a change of heart and put the house back on the market. The "for sale" sign seems to be perpetually stuck in the front lawn.

Ever wonder why that home is always for sale?

Simple. It's haunted.

New people move in to the home and get spooked. Then they immediately put the house up for sale again.

Students at the University of Maryland who wonder why departments and offices continually move in—and out—of Morrill Hall now have an answer. Morrill Hall, built in 1898, is haunted. It's one of the most haunted buildings on Maryland's superhaunted campus.

It's the haunted vibe that people notice as soon as they walk though Morrill's halls. People describe it as a heavy, overwhelming feeling. But it's more than just a bad vibe. After all, that could easily be ascribed to an overactive imagination. Morrill Hall is paranormally overactive.

Workers, for instance, continually complain about hearing noises late at night.

Then, there are those strange accidents. People—who are not normally klutzy folks—say they unexpectedly trip and fall. Or are they tripped by some of Morrill Hall's pushy spirits?

So, is there a source of the strange activity behind the activity at Morrill Hall and a reason for the constant shuffling in and out of university personnel? A prank-loving frat boy? A klutzy coed?

The university website has one suggestion. Apparently, a few years ago, a group of workers who were helping renovate Morrill found some human remains under a sink.

That'll do it.

Remains that are improperly buried are right up there with Ouija boards and murder-suicides on the list of how properties get haunted.

There's no word on whether any student group or paranormal-research association has tried to calm down the spirits who haunt Morrill. It seems that university staff and students have learned to live with and—actually—love their friends from the otherworld, even when they turn into pranksters.

## Marie Mount Hall—University of Maryland
### *A Deeper Exploration of Haunted Home Economics*

Marie Mount Hall was named for one of the University of Maryland's most famous faculty members. She was the first dean of the College of Home Economics. It's a duty she didn't take lightly. When she passed on to the other side, a part of her spirit remained in Marie Mount Hall to begin a whole new career as dean of the College of Haunted Home Economics.

Stories of ghostly encounters at the building are common. Some might be passed around as fun campus tales for the students, but some of the staff claim there's serious haunting going around the halls of

Marie Mount Hall. And when Halloween comes around, the nerves of employees are particularly on edge.

A secretary told one student investigator that on Halloween night the piano that Marie supposedly played during her career at the University of Maryland suddenly cranks out tunes all by itself, spooking the staff.

"No they don't like to be around," the secretary reported. "Nobody likes to be around because of that. Everyone that you talk to, they'll say the same thing."

Some people don't need to hear the Halloween piano concerto to be reminded of the ghost that haunts Marie Mount Hall; the picture of Marie that hangs in the main hall appears to keep a close eye on students and staff. The picture's eyes seem to follow you, no matter where you are in the room.

An apparition of Marie has been spotted around the building, too, lending more evidence to the idea that Marie Mount Hall is more than just another campus legend. It's the real supernatural deal. A medium who was called in to investigate Marie Mount Hall said she made contact with the ghost of Marie Mount.

Her conclusion: Marie Mount Hall is haunted.

Really haunted.

## H. J. Patterson Hall—University of Maryland

*Terror for a Terrapin*

If you thought it was scary to work at Marie Mount Hall, welcome to H. J. Patterson Hall.

One employee found out that the hard way that the campus landmark is also a haunted landmark.

According to the account, a staff member who was part of facilities management was working alone in H. J. Patterson Hall, an impressive campus building also known as Steinberg Castle. The worker was facing the wall when a shadow inexplicably drifted across the wall.

It may have been quick, but it left a lasting impression on the employee.

This story is just one documented report that corroborates lots of chatter that the building is another addition to the list of University of Maryland's paranormal spots.

The ghost of Patterson is a bit of a mystery. No one seems to know the source of the haunting. It might be the ghost of Henry Jacob Patterson, who was a pioneer in agricultural education.

The Engineering Department also used the building. Maybe they engineered some paranormal activity at Patterson.

## Winslow Hall—North Carolina State
### *Do Ghosts Still Haunt the Site of the Infamous Infirmary?*

It surrounds you as soon as you walk into Winslow Hall. It's a feeling that's hard to describe. Some say they feel sad. Some feel consumed by loss. Others claim they sense unseen eyes watching them as they work.

But, it's far more than just a feeling.

If any of NC State's buildings have a reason to be haunted, it's Winslow Hall.

The building was constructed in 1897 and was once used as the campus infirmary. Most campus infirmaries face the typical ills and accidents that affect college kids—bumps, bruises, colds, and the occasional hangover.

But, in 1918, things got serious at the Winslow Hall infirmary. Deadly serious.

The influenza epidemic that swept through the nation in the early twentieth century took direct aim at NC State's campus. With the swiftness of its onset and the ferocity of its symptoms, the epidemic stretched the limits of the university's ability to care for the students. The sick were transported to the infirmary where the doctors, nurses, and staff members who volunteered to help worked round-the-clock to save as many students as possible. One of those volunteers was the daughter of the University's Chancellor Wallace Riddick at the time.

The chancellor's daughter, along with 13 students perished from influenza. Things were never the same at Winslow Hall after the epidemic, as you can imagine. Students and staff say Winslow is haunted with the restless spirits of the victims of the influenza outbreak. The basement apparently is the most haunted spot in the building.

Most of the accounts of paranormal activity come from employees who worked in Winslow Hall and who spent most of their time there.

Spaine Stephens, who worked in the building in the late 1990s, told the student newspaper, the *Technician*, that she felt some strange vibes while working there. She felt, at times, like someone was watching her work. Oddly, Stephens sensed that the spirit, or spirits, who watched her were also interested in her work. They weren't trying to scare her off.

"It was by no means a threatening feeling," Stephens said. "If anything, as soon as I started feeling like I was being watched, I got a sad, nostalgic feeling, maybe like the people who died there felt."

Her fellow workers told her that they had more than feelings that spirits were near; they saw and heard the ghosts that walked the halls of Winslow. At times, they heard something moving around overhead. The coworkers, too, suspected the haunting was connected to the influenza epidemic.

"They said they felt like the presence they felt was connected to the deaths from the 1918 flu that happened when that building was the infirmary."

At NC State, 1918 was a bad year for spooks. But how does it compare to 1911?

## 1911 Building—North Carolina State
### *Is 1911 the Date Named After a Famous NC State Class or the Number of Ghosts that Lie Within?*

Every class that enters NC State is special. Faculty will tell you that each class has its own personality. The faculty who were teaching at NC State in 1911 sensed something different about the class of 1911. Like other universities, it was a tradition for upperclassmen to haze incoming freshmen. The hazings ranged from intense discipline to humiliating initiation rites.

The class of 1911 had enough of hazing and vowed to end the humiliation.

Faculty considered it a "landmark in the history of the college." When a new 45,000 square-foot Victorian dormitory was built, the university's professors and members of the administration named the building after the class that dared to stop the nasty practice of hazing.

The hazing may have stopped. The tales of haunting haven't.

Students who have walked through the elegant Victorian dormitory at night hear footsteps following after them. It's enough to creep out the most skeptical student and, according to one account, even campus security doesn't like the nightly visit to the 1911 Building. During the campus ghost walk, one campus police officer escorting the group told the tour when they stopped at the 1911 Building that, even today, certain officers refuse to enter the building.

Maybe they hear the footsteps, too?

## Spring Hill House—North Carolina State
*Former Plantation, Civil War Hospital, Graveyard*

NC State's research campus is called its Centennial Campus. The campus is known for leading-edge research. Engineering marvels, researching biomedical cures, and innovating the latest green technologies are just a few examples of its latest work.

I forgot one other thing that buildings in the Centennial Campus are known for: capturing ghosts with high-tech surveillance equipment.

The Spring Hill House, now the NC Japan Center, has a haunted pedigree that stretches back into the nineteenth century. It was a former plantation house that eventually became part of the North Carolina State system. Like every good haunted house, there's a grave nearby, too. The grave of Col. Theophilus Hunter, Sr.—which just happens to be the oldest marked grave in Durham County—rests a few hundred feet from the stately building. This might be one reason for the Spring Hill House's haunted rap sheet.

Historians also suggest that the property has witnessed its share of tragedy. Tens of thousands of Confederate troops camped nearby and may have even commandeered the house as a hospital.

Over the years, security officers report that something trips the motion detectors in the building, but when officers arrive on the scene a few moments later, there's nothing there. Skeptics would point out that it could be an animal that trips the device or some sort of faulty wiring, but the incidents occurred with such frequency that the rumors of paranormal activity began to grow.

The current residents said the building has been quiet lately and offer a reason.

Tony Moyer, associate director of the NC Japan Center, told a reporter from the *Technician*, "We were new occupants. The ghost didn't know us, so whoever it is wanted to see what kinds of books we had on the bookshelves and learn what we were up to, but it hasn't bothered us since."

## Old Main—University of Arizona
### *Knock, Knock, Knocking on Heaven's Door?*

You would expect a few ghosts to be lurking around the University of Arizona's Old Main. It's old. It's historic. And, after all, doesn't every campus have a supernatural rumor or legend about its founding buildings?

And firsthand accounts indicate that the haunting of Old Main is not just rumor and innuendo.

Andy Martinez, a custodian who worked the late-night shift at Old Main, told the *Arizona Daily Wildcat* that he became a believer.

As an employee, Martinez had heard the rumors that Old Main was haunted. He even witnessed some strange activity. On a couple occasions, securely fastened clocks mysteriously exploded off the walls.

He also heard the water fountains recharge, even though he knew he was the only one in the building. Most paranormal researchers would consider this behavior to be manifestations of a poltergeist, a German term for "noisy spirit." Poltergeist activity is typically connected to the unconscious telekinetic powers of a living human, not a spirit who has passed on.

While those poltergeist episodes gave him pause, another incident convinced the custodian that Old Main has ghosts.

Martinez said he was in the building alone one night. It was around 10 p.m. and Martinez was next to a wall on the second floor when he heard distinct knocking. He stood still and looked around. Since all the doors were locked, Martinez was hoping that the strange knock was just someone knocking on the glass door at the building's entrance. He checked that door out. No one was there.

A second distinct knock sounded.

Martinez said he just stood there and then a third knock erupted.

He told the *Daily Wildcat*: "And I was like, 'Wait a minute, I know I'm not hearing things.'"

Martinez yelled out to the source of the knocking to come in. Suddenly, the knocking stopped.

Now, perhaps wondering exactly what he let in, Martinez said he gets chills whenever he passes the spot.

As the stories of haunted Old Main continue, the custodian apparently isn't the only one creeped out in the university's older building.

## The Farm House—Iowa State University
### *All Hail that Prairie Pioneer Spirit*

The Farm House, built in the 1860s, is the oldest standing structure on the Iowa State University campus and, arguably, the most famous landmark for the Cyclone faithful. It's currently used as a museum, but it truly serves as an architectural testament to the rugged, pioneer spirit of both the people of Iowa, who helped found the school, and the students and faculty who continue to work to make the school and the world a better place.

The ghost—or ghosts—of the Farm House, though, are just as legendary.

The haunting of the Farm House all started, legend has it, with Edith Curtiss, the daughter of the College of Agriculture's dean during the early days of the university. Edith and her dad were among the earliest, if not the earliest, tenants of the house. Edith's room was situated on the second floor. She was often seen standing at the windows with the curtains drawn aside. Word had it that she had a beau or two among the male student body and would wait pensively for their appearance at the house.

She's still waiting, according to one curator of the Farm House. The curator said that before leaving she made sure she closed the curtains on the second floor. At least she thought she did. When the curator arrived at work the next morning, the curtains were wide open. That day, before she left work, she double- and even triple-checked that the curtains were closed. When she was outside, the curator even looked back at the Farm House to make sure the curtains were close.

They were. But not for long.

The next morning, the curtains were open again. This time, the curtains weren't just gently pushed to the side; they appeared to be violently drawn apart.

The curator was stumped. Maybe it was the wind, she decided—or hoped. She concocted a plan to get the answer. This time, before she exited the building for the night, she made sure to stitch the curtains closed with pins. Maybe that would stop the breeze—or whatever force—was blowing the curtains open.

The next morning, the curator arrived expecting to see the pins securely fastened and the curtains drawn firmly closed. Standing in front of the Farm House, the curator looked at the second-floor window and saw the curtains were pushed aside. She ran to the second floor and saw the pins—that she had so meticulously used to bind the curtains together—were lying on the floor.

Edith had won that battle.

More recently, other curators, employees, and visitors have stepped forward to tell stories of their encounters with Edith, or whoever is haunting the Farm House. A university employee named Allison charged with keeping an eye on the Farm House while the curator was on vacation told the student newspaper, the *Iowa State Daily*, of one such encounter.

Before leaving for the day, Allison set the dining room table with a new tablecloth and new dishes. The spirits were not amused. Allison had a rude surprise the next morning. The dishes weren't just moved or pushed aside; they were tossed around the dining room.

There had to be a natural explanation, she thought. It could be college pranksters. But why would they just mess with a set of dishes in the out-of-the-way dining room and not attack some of the other rooms and displays?

Allison dutifully gathered the dishes together and re-set the table.

The next morning, the dining room was in disarray. The dishes were scattered across the room and the tablecloth was askew. Standing in the midst of the wreckage, the employee finally summoned the nerve to tell the boss what happened. Sometimes summoning the courage to face down an angry spirit is more difficult than facing a skeptical superior, but the employee gave her boss the blow-by-blow account of the events. The boss ordered a structural examination of the building. Was it possible that the house was settling violently?

Predictably, that wasn't the case.

While the whole episode was written off as a prank or a natural phenomena—although, let's face it, a highly unlikely natural phenomena—whispers among the staff and students tend to have other ideas about what caused the ruckus at the Farm House: the ghost of Edith Curtiss. As if those accounts weren't evidence enough, reports still trickle in about flickering lights and wandering objects to further confirm the house's status as most haunted place on campus.

There's one other sign that proves people believe the Farm House is haunted. Nobody touches Edith's curtains or moves her silverware anymore.

## The Cathedral of Learning—University of Pittsburgh
### *It's More Like the Cathedral of Haunting*

The Cathedral of Learning isn't your typical campus building; it's a towering tribute to both the city of Pittsburgh and to the belief that higher education can make the world a better place.

It's supposedly the second-largest educational building in the world, but the building is without a doubt the tallest haunted educational building.

Hands down.

The Cathedral of Learning opened in 1937 after a nearly 10-year construction project that progressed during the Great Depression, a bleak time for Pittsburgh and the world. The structure that soars 535 feet above the Oakland neighborhood was more than a college building—it was a symbol of life. In the words of Pitt Chancellor John Gabbert Bowman:

"The building was to be more than a schoolhouse; it was to be a symbol of the life that Pittsburgh through the years had wanted to live. It was to make visible something of the spirit that was in the hearts of pioneers as, long ago, they sat in their log cabins and thought by candlelight of the great city that would sometime spread out beyond their three rivers and that even they were starting to build."

Some of the Pitt faithful will tell you that the Cathedral wasn't just a symbol of life, it also become a symbol of death—and what lies beyond this life.

Maybe some of the mystery that this skyscraper inspires is based on the architectural style. It's a Gothic Revival masterpiece and Gothic architecture, of course, has an ethereal, otherworldly quality. Reflecting this ornate style, the Cathedral is made of steel and limestone and contains approximately 2,000 rooms and more than 2,500 windows.

And a couple of ghosts, too.

The Cathedral of Learning has museum-like rooms dedicated to the cultures that helped build Pittsburgh and its namesake university. One of those rooms on the Cathedral's third floor has been dubbed the Early American Room, and one spirit is said to haunt it.

The Early American Room gives visitors an idea of what life would be like during those early Colonial times, when Pittsburgh was barely a village and the University of Pittsburgh was just a twinkle in the eye of some founder. A fireplace and all the accoutrement—hooks, kettles, a gridiron, a waffle iron, a bread shovel, and ladles and forks—are on display. Pine beams were brought in from Massachusetts and the dining table and chairs are a stunning example of furniture made from white pine.

But underneath all this austere, stoic sixteenth-century living, there is a mystery—a secret panel that you can find between a blackboard and the fireplace. Once it's unlatched, the wall swings open and a hidden staircase leads to a loft that is furnished as a seventeenth-century bedroom. The bedroom is outfitted with a handmade wedding quilt that experts date to the 1850s. A pine crib is nearby, as are an antique Bible and a wash set.

Paranormal experts say that room is kept off limits—accessed only through a secret passage—for one very important reason. It's haunted. The experts add that there are almost as many ghostly suspects for this haunting as there are floors in this towering tribute to education.

If you want to verify the haunting, you have to talk to people who have the most unfettered access to the room. The best folks to query are the custodians, who have the unenviable task of cleaning and maintaining the strange, secretive room. These workers are there day and night. It's night when things get interesting, most of the custodians say.

One custodian offers this tale. He said he made his way to the secret room and was horrified to find the quilt folded like someone had just slept—or maybe was sleeping—in the bed. There was even an indentation in the pillow that formed an outline of a human head. It wasn't the last time this spectral sleeper visited the bedroom. Since then, other visitors have claimed to see the quilt move ever so slightly or have noticed that strange indentation in the blanket and pillow.

The creepy cradle in the Early American Room gives birth to even more stories of paranormal activity. Witnesses report walking into the room and seeing the cradle gently rock like an invisible hand is lulling an invisible child to sleep. You can almost hear the lullaby, they say.

Unseen cradle rockers and phantom nappers are only the start of the paranormal phenomena reported in the Nationality Rooms. In one incident, a Cathedral tour guide had a run-in with a hungry ghost; or, more accurately, a ghost that made her hungry.

While walking through the Early American Room, the guide said she smelled the unmistakable—and delicious—scent of fresh-baked bread. Since there isn't a bakery near the room and no one in the room had fresh bread in hand, the guide assumed that the smell was the ghostly remnant of times—perhaps supper times—past.

Paranormal experts would probably classify the scent as a twist on a "residual haunting." While most residuals are filmy images of ghosts repeating the same actions over and over again, experts suggest that there can also be phantom noises—and even smells.

That's merely a scratch on the surface of the Nationality Rooms' haunted legacy. For more than three decades, the rooms that explore Pittsburgh's unique cultural milieu have also provided people a glimpse of Pitt's paranormal tapestry.

Frequently, people have complained about sudden shifts in temperature as they tour the rooms. There are reports that the temperatures suddenly drop without any observable cause—no open windows, no air conditioner springing to life, etc. This is a common sign of spectral guests. Researchers suggest that to manifest, spirits draw energy from the surrounding environment. The result is a temperature drop in the immediate vicinity.

In a more dramatic demonstration of supernatural power, one tour group witnessed a candle flame inexplicably flared up as they neared it. Maybe that will teach people to stop complaining about the cold spots ...

Cold spots and paranormal pyrotechnics aren't the only phenomena that send shivers down the spines of guests. A long line of witnesses have come forward to claim that they have seen chilling apparitions of a mysterious entity who is considered a permanent resident of the Cathedral of Learning. A psychic visiting the Cathedral said she saw the ghost. She described it as a woman with her hair pulled back and wearing an apron.

A maintenance worker recently told of a more frightening encounter with the same ghost. Responsible for cleaning the room and locking the doors, the employee said that as he climbed the stairs to complete his duties, he saw a dark shadow near the bed.

"It came out of the room and disappeared in front of me," he told a *Pittsburgh Post-Gazette* reporter.

His fellow workers vouch for the custodian's honesty and they say he's telling the truth. One janitor was right behind the man when his coworker ran into the shadow person. She said the janitor was visibly spooked (literally) and he's difficult to rattle.

## Spirit Suspects

The theories about the origin of the Cathedral's haunted activity are vast and diverse. The haunting is a poltergeist. It's a residual energy. It's an active spirit. And, for each of these theories, there seem to be just as many spirit suspects who are said to be behind both the Cathedral and Nationality Rooms' paranormal activity.

Tragedies, like murders and deadly accidents, get blamed for causing most hauntings. But, the Cathedral doesn't have an obvious history of such events. A few paranormal researchers speculate that the building isn't haunted, or even the room. It may be that common everyday objects are causing the haunting, especially in the Early American Room haunting. These investigators base this theory on the idea that in most ghost stories, there can be a tie between an object and an emotional event or events that create the activity.

The bed, the quilt, and some of the other pieces of furniture on display in the room certainly seem to be connected with the paranormal action in the Cathedral.

These objects are original and in their 300-plus years of existence may have absorbed their share of trauma and psychic energy, paranormal researchers suggest. According to this haunted-object theory, these objects take this energy—and paranormal activity—with them wherever they go.

Oddly enough, the quilt that some say is the source of the haunted activity was passed down to Pitt from the family of Maxine Bruhns, a historian and a leading expert of the Nationality Rooms. Maxine, who serves as the second director of the Nationality Rooms, told the writer in *Original Magazine* (a magazine dedicated to Pittsburgh's artists and arts) that the bed has a blanket that was once owned by her West Virginia grandmother, Martha Jane Poe.

The irony isn't lost on paranormal researchers. Martha, after all, is a distant relative of horror master Edgar Allan Poe. Maxine, for one, believes that it may just be her grandmother—a relative of Edgar Allan Poe—who haunts the room.

When leading tours, Bruhns asks visitors to remain quiet and respectful, just in case the ghost decides to join them on the tour. The technique often works.

Bruhns says she has had several encounters with either her grandmother's ghost or a poltergeist that inhabits the space.

She told the *Pittsburgh Post-Gazette* that one time she firmly placed several dried ears of corn on a peg to the left of the fireplace. Without warning or visible cause, the corn exploded off the peg, sending a shower of kernels around the room.

Bruhns said the corn was firmly secured on the four-inch nail. And there was no way that an animal was responsible for removing the corn from the crib.

In another incident of possible poltergeist activity, Bruhns said she discovered that a photograph of her grandmother at age 16 had been cracked. No one had an explanation why the photograph was cracked—it was carefully packed and stored to prevent just such an accident.

The "corn saga" and cracked photograph, which have become legendary incidents in the Cathedral's extensive paranormal history, are nothing compared to Maxine Bruhns's next brush with the spirit of her grandmother.

Bruhns said that one night she decided to call her grandmother out and asked her to reveal herself. Maybe not her best idea.

Her story goes like this:

She was staying overnight in the Nationality Room. (Now there's a brave woman for you.) The room was pitch black and silent. Bruhns rolled out her sleeping bag at the foot of the infamous rope bed. Then something moved her to reach out into the unknown.

Into the darkness, Bruhns yelled out, "I'm here, Grandma! I'm alone now if you want to contact me."

There was silence at first. But, as Bruhns drifted off to sleep, an odd "swishing" sound stirred her from her sleep. She waited in the dark silence. The noise fluttered by her again!

Was this her grandmother's answer?

Suddenly something crashed down beside her.

Bruhns's courage began to crumble as she lay motionless, too scared to move. Finally, summoning all the inner strength she had available, she grabbed the flashlight and scanned the room.

She found that a water bottle she had placed securely in her overnight bag had somehow levitated out of her bag and fallen off the chair.

Bruhns did not believe it was an accident or a coincidence.

She yelled out to her grandma again, "Grandma, you can have this damn room!"

While Bruhns asks visitors to remain respectful on their tour of the Nationality Rooms, they should be reminded to keep quiet and respectful throughout the Cathedral because rumor has it the building is packed full of those ghostly presences.

## No Rest for the Romantic

Another supernatural presence people say they have encountered in the Cathedral of Learning is Mary Croghan Schenley. Mary walks the halls of the Nationality Rooms and, if accounts are correct, she might even swing off the chandeliers in the ballroom. Once you get to know the real Mary Croghan Schenley, you'll realize that swinging off the chandeliers isn't out of the question for one of our nation's pioneering party girls.

If the name, "Schenley," seems familiar, it's because the name is attached to numerous Pittsburgh landmarks and more than a few places at the University of Pittsburgh, like Schenley Hall. And Mary wouldn't have minded at all. She did a pretty good job of spreading the Schenley name around when she was alive.

Mary was the granddaughter and only heir of the vast tracts of land owned by her maternal grandfather and Pittsburgh businessman, James O'Hara. Rich and romantic, she soon made a name for herself in the scandal sheets of her day. As a student at a Staten Island boarding school, Mary fell in love with a 43-year-old British Army captain named Edward Wyndham Harrington Schenley. They eloped.

Mary was only 15 at the time, and a firestorm of disappointment and shame spread across the Atlantic as the couple sought refuge in England. To make matters worse, this was the third elopement for the good captain.

Mary's rich father threatened to cut his daughter off entirely if she went through with the marriage.

Luckily, the third time would be a charm for the captain and his young, wealthy bride.

Mary's father may have not liked the arrangement, but he had a soft heart for his little girl. When the couple became destitute, he had a change of heart and accepted his daughter back into the family fold. Mary resided in London mostly, but she was generous with the loads of money and land she inherited back in America. Most of the land was donated to Pittsburgh, its churches, institutions, and schools, including the University of Pittsburgh and the plot of land that the Cathedral now rests on.

Is Mary's vivacious spirit prompting the Cathedral's haunting? Maybe. But there are more theories to examine.

Another legend is that it's not a person who's haunting the Cathedral of Learning, it's an object or objects. This theory points out that several items from Croghan-Schenley Ballroom could be stirring up the paranormal forces.

The ballroom is located on the first floor and, like the rest of the Cathedral, has its share of mysteries. For instance, the room has a hidden passageway in the fireplace that connects it with the adjoining Oval Room. The rooms were originally part of William Croghan Jr.'s mansion, but were painstakingly removed and restored in the Cathedral when a demolition project threatened to level the mansion.

In 1945, *Life* magazine actually featured the story about the restoration project. The title of the article was "Life Visits a Haunted House."

The refurbished rooms are dominated by a hand-cut glass chandelier. The chandelier, which also is said to have proudly hung in Mary's mansion, is an ornate example of craftsmanship. It's also amazingly haunted. Witnesses have seen the chandelier begin to shake. At other times, it sways. There is no breeze, these witnesses say. Nor does there seem to be any vibrations causing the disturbance—at least, vibrations of the mundane, earthly sort. If there is a vibration, it doesn't disturb any other objects in the room. Witnesses say that even when they see the chandelier sway, they notice that papers don't flutter, hair doesn't blow, and the furniture remains in place.

At other times, Mary engages in some of her own restoration efforts.

In one of the more extreme examples of paranormal activity in the Cathedral of Learning, the beds have been unmade and the furniture has been rearranged, even though the night crew had locked all the doors. Members of the terrified day crew who have witnessed the odd redecoration efforts claim there is no natural explanation for the actions that include dramatic moves of large, heavy objects and furniture.

In her life, Mary was used to inspiring debate. Things haven't changed. She's the center of a debate among the paranormal community and those who study folklore at Pitt. Some say Mary, alone, is the sole ghost involved in the Nationality Rooms' paranormal reputation, but others say she's just one of many spirits.

On the other hand, the haunting might not have anything to do with old quilts or swinging chandeliers, or even swinging heiresses, say other students familiar with the haunting of the skyscraping Cathedral; it might be that the ghost in the Early American Room just needs a drink to wash down all that fresh-baked bread.

## *Cathedral's Creepy Cafeteria*
### WANDERING SOUL FOOD

Ever since John Belushi screamed the immortal collegiate cafeteria cheer, "food fight," and chucked his plate of food across the cafeteria room, college food has become the stuff of both legend and derision.

The problem at the Cathedral of Learning isn't bad food or food fights. By all accounts, the food in the Cathedral notches up rave reviews. The place even has a sushi bar! There doesn't seem to be a tradition of tossing food at your cafeteria mates, either.

The source of the trouble in the cafeteria doesn't seem to come from the staff, either. The cooks, servers, and clean-up crews get kudos from diners.

It's the spirit visitors who frequent the cafeteria that freak out students and workers on a regular occasion.

The Cathedral's cafeteria is just one more paranormal power spot in the building, according to several accounts. Many of these stories of spirit encounters and brushes with the weird come from cafeteria workers.

Workers say these strange happenings usually occur at night and usually at off-hours when the cafeteria is really dead—so to speak. At the top of the cafeteria's supernatural menu is a heaping-helping of poltergeist activity. Witnesses watch horrified as carts start to move by themselves—on a perfectly level floor, they're quick to add. Then, there are tales of an unseen hand pushing boxes along the floor. At other times, this spirit spins the boxes.

The power that propels this poltergeist activity in the cafeteria may be the same force that causes workers to say they can sense something walking by them late at night. It's an eerie feeling, like a breeze or a blast of air. But, unlike a draft or stray breeze, the workers believe this force has a purpose. They call it a presence.

And sometimes, the workers report, this presence can pass right through you.

Another sign of ghostly activity in the cafeteria is a chilling reminder of the spirit world that haunts the Cathedral. Witnesses have seen the handle of an ice machine suddenly depress and splatter ice cubes all over the floor.

While cynics quickly point out that a faulty ice machine could cause the spill, a few reports indicate that people have seen the handle actually move, as if a person—that no one can see—was pushing on it.

## *The Search Continues…*

Education is a search for answers and a way to confront the unknown. These seekers—teachers and students—are determined to explore subjects that were once objects of both fear and curiosity, from the depths of the earth to the unfathomable stretches of deep space.

This desire to explore led to "science"—a rigorous, methodical examination of the unknown.

But there's one source of the unknown that appears safely tucked away from the powerful punches of science and education: that mysterious field where life settles after death. While there are those who walk on the Pitt campus who purportedly have a solution—ignore it. For them, if science can't measure it, it doesn't exist. They don't believe in ghosts or spirits. Poltergeists have a natural explanation. End of story.

But for others, it's the accounts of ghostly visitors and unexplained phenomena of the unknown that echo from the Cathedral of Learning and other parts of the university that make ignoring the unknown impossible for others.

Cafeteria workers, custodians, curators, and students who have spent nights in the long, dark halls of the Cathedral of Learning have an answer to skeptics: spend a night in the Cathedral.

Spending some time at night in this Cathedral of the Unknown, they say, is a life-changing and possibly even a death-altering experience.

# Alumni Hall—University of Pittsburgh
## The Paranormal Pitt Code

Alumni Hall was not always a temple of higher education.

It was another type of temple.

In the early part of the twentieth century, the imposing limestone building that rests on Fifth Avenue (near the Cathedral) at Pitt was used as a Masonic Temple. Masons, if you follow the reams of conspiracy theories, did not just possess the secrets of building, they possessed the secrets of magic.

Masonic secrets are passed on to members and followers through a range of mysterious rituals. These rituals were once performed in the temple long before it became Pitt's Alumni Hall. Students now wonder if the residual magic left over from those days as a hall of secret rites and rituals is now causing Alumni Hall's current haunted activity.

Those witnesses who have seen a solitary wisp of a figure slide down the cavernous halls of the building don't need to wonder. They know the hall is haunted.

Whether the building has always had ghosts is unknown. The activity seemed to spark as soon as Pitt purchased the building in the early 1990s to create Alumni Hall. Architects are particularly impressed with features, like the ornamental terra cotta pediment and clay tile roof that make the building look like a classic temple.

With an extensive renovation effort, the university transformed Masonic Temple into a veritable temple of Pitt glory. It's a place where alumni could bask in the academic and athletic prowess of their alma mater. The building was eventually added to the Pittsburgh History and Landmark Foundation's list of historic landmarks in the city.

The Pitt Alumni Association, which now makes its home in the building, is the official keeper of the gloried past of Pitt's many alumni standouts. The Legacy Gallery in Alumni Hall, currently housed on the first floor, offers interactive kiosks for people to explore alumni, faculty, and student achievements.

The virtual archive, which serves as an electronic exploration into Pitt's history and history-makers, isn't the only reminder of the past. According to reports, several witnesses have seen a ghost in Alumni Hall.

Most stories about the Alumni Hall ghost come from folks who were walking through the building after hours or before the mad rush of workers and visitors who arrive each morning. Witnesses, who are usually alone, say they're walking down the silent, empty halls when they see a figure out of the corner of their eyes.

The ghost has been described as a man clad in a black tuxedo. (There must be formal occasions in the afterlife.) The man emerges from a shadowy corner and heads toward one of the stairwells. His gait has been described as an eerie glide, not a walk.

Most witnesses report being so stunned that they can't move. Only the truly brave follow the man. According to one story, a witness chased after the figure and said the ghost faded away as he walked down the steps. And disappeared.

So, who is this impeccably attired spirit?

No one knows.

He doesn't seem to resemble any of the officials, administrators, legendary sports heroes, or other people from Pitt's past who might want to continue to linger around the alumni headquarters.

The figure doesn't look like any of past Pittsburgh's famous historic figures, either. He doesn't resemble Andrew Carnegie, Henry Clay Frick, Thomas Mellon, Charles Schwab, or other Pittsburgh pioneers.

People most familiar with the ghostly lore of the Steel City have one guess, though—they believe this well-dressed spirit is the ghost of a lost Mason. Perhaps, he is trapped between the world of the living and the dead. Or maybe he's a little confused that his Masonic Temple has become the new Pitt alumni facility.

Or, is this spirit just one more secret that the ancient order of Masons refuses to divulge?

Secrets abound on the University of Pittsburgh campus.

## Crosley Tower—University of Cincinnati

*The Tower of Supernatural Power*

There's no polite way to say this. Most of the students aren't afraid of walking near the Crosley Tower because it's haunted, they're afraid of walking near the tower because it's ugly. The unusual design predominates the skyline of the University of Cincinnati campus. It's earned a reputation as one of the ugliest buildings on campus, but architects are far more generous. They describe the style of the 16-floor building as Brutalist.

When you hear the ghost story that takes place at Crosley, Brutalist takes on a whole new meaning.

According to Greg Hand, a university spokesman who talked with the University of Cincinnati student newspaper, a few rumors have circulated about the tower.

The most famous—and the most disturbing—originated before the building opened. Workers feverishly toiled to have the tower completed by the deadline. It wasn't an easy task. The unique design of the tower required expert workmanship. As a group of construction workers poured the concrete that would be used in forming the building, one worker slipped in. They couldn't save him. The rumor is that the body is still encased in the building.

Paranormal researchers would suggest that this type of horrific accident could spawn a haunting.

Hand says that the story isn't true. No one ever died during the building's construction. But, true or not, students say weird things happen in Crosley Tower. Students claim they can hear a gentle sighing. Others say the construction worker still walks the halls of Crosley—looking for a way out.

If a worker was not killed at the tower, could these students be imaging things? Or lying? Or, could it be even more complex?

Paranormal researchers suggest an urban legend can actually germinate a real ghost. According to this theory, concentrated thought can actually cause real paranormal activity. A poltergeist—which has been documented to move and disturb objects—may be the result of the intense emotional state of a person in the house or building. These agents, as they're often called, can somehow transfer this anger or fear into the environment, usually in bursts of strange phenomena. Cups will fly off tables. Drawers will open. Books will slide across shelves. The activity is nearly unlimited.

Researchers suggest, then, that if enough people believe a story and imprint their own beliefs onto an environment, a ghost—or ghostly activity—could appear.

Is this what's going on at the tower?

It's hard to say, but most students are not afraid of the ghost of the construction worker. In fact, they kind of pity him. After all, could you imagine being stuck in such an ugly building for an eternity?

# The Ridges—Ohio University

*Ghosts Attached to Site of Former Mental Institution*

At Ohio University, students don't need esoteric theories of spontaneous paranormal activity to believe in the supernatural. The campus is full of evidence.

By all accounts, the Athens Insane Asylum, commonly known as The Ridges, was a successful and humane place for the mentally ill in the late eighteenth and early nineteenth century. The asylum was actually a complex of buildings and gardens that were welcomed by the citizens of Athens, who saw it as a boost to their economy. In fact, there was a rash of insane asylum building in several cities of Ohio, but don't read too much into this as a statement on the mental stability of the people of Ohio.

The Athens Insane Asylum, in its time a brilliantly successful experiment in the treatment of the mentally ill, began to fall victim of its success, critics say. The asylum grew overcrowded. People would drop off elderly relatives who they were tired of caring for, and parents sent rebellious teenagers to Athens for minor disciplinary infractions. Meanwhile, more "active" treatments of the mentally ill, including lobotomy surgery, were carried out in the asylum with debatable success.

The overcrowded conditions led to a crumbling of services and sanitation. Eventually, the asylum was closed and the property sold to Ohio University, which had plans to refurbish and convert the buildings into a museum, classrooms, and administrative space.

But while those plans progressed, the students of Ohio University had a chance to reconnoiter their newly acquired campus properties. When they reported back to their classmates, the word wasn't good. The university, it seemed, had bought buildings that were already occupied—occupied by ghosts.

They encountered one of the weirdest paranormal artifacts. On the third floor, the students discovered the perfect outline of a woman's body.

It became known, simply and accurately, as the stain.

Several explanations were proffered for the stain, but one story stuck.

The story goes that an inmate named Margaret Schilling wandered into a room that was being refurbished in what is now called Lin Hall. Workers who had finished their section of the renovation locked the door behind them, not knowing that Marge was still inside. A massive search was organized, but the search party never thought to look in the locked third-floor room. And, curiously, they never heard Marge's cries for help.

Weeks later, a horrible stench led searchers to the worst-case discovery. Marge was found lying lifeless on the floor. When the body was removed, the medical team found the strange outline. Even more troubling, the stain could not be removed.

But the stain isn't the only residue left in The Ridges; there's plenty of psychic residue in the facility.

Recently, a group of freshman students were working on a paranormal film as a class project. They began filming outside of one of the basement windows at The Ridges. While they filmed, none of the students saw anything peculiar. They moved on.

Later, though, as they edited their film, they discovered something that chilled the students to the bone.

During the scene filmed at the basement window, a pale figure appears in the foreground. No one saw the figure there during filming.

D. J. Hill, one of the students on the shoot, explained, "I don't know if it's a ghost caught on tape, but it's something."

Other students have seen and heard that "something."

And they see and hear that something all over campus.

## Wilson Hall—Ohio University
### *The Most Haunted of the Most Haunted*

Here's a little multiple choice exam for the haunting of Wilson Hall.

Wilson Hall, one of Ohio University's most infamous buildings, is haunted because:

1. It's located right at the geographic center of Ohio University's mysterious cemetery pentagram.

2. A student may have inadvertently brought spirits to Wilson Hall after she touched "the stain" at The Ridges.

3. It doesn't need a reason to be haunted; just being built in haunted Athens, Ohio, is reason enough.

4. The dorm was built on the site of native American burial ground.

5. All of the above.

Read on for the answer...

When the film crew for Fox Family Channel's *Scariest Places on Earth* scouted Ohio University for the perfect backdrop for an episode, they stopped the search right after visiting Wilson Hall.

It's just one of those buildings that looks haunted. Long and stately, the building seems like it holds a haunted legend or two. Maybe three.

Okay, possibly five.

The first legend is that a student who was living at Wilson started to exhibit some strange behavior after she began her stay at the dorm. She started to chant and sing in a strange language. Her friends became concerned, but before they could intervene, the story is, she jumped out of the window and killed herself.

Her room, Room 428, has been closed since, they say. And the entire dorm has been haunted.

The paranormal episodes range from the small—and a little silly—to what experts would call, "megaparanormal" activity.

The little stuff—strange noises and the occasional electromagnetic disturbance, like a light that turns on and off by itself—are easy to explain naturally. It could be student pranks or bad wiring. The other stuff isn't so easy to dismiss.

Students who roomed in Wilson Hall say that they've seen furniture move. These were big pieces of furniture, too—desks and dresses. Books and knick-knacks fly off of shelves. There are also stories of doors that open and close, with no one near them.

Advocates of the "Wilson Hall" is haunted theory tend to divide into two camps. One group backs the "weird-chanting coed" theory. Another group says that the female student wasn't the victim of a random spiritual demise, these believers say that the victim was driven to suicide after she touched "the stain" at the Ridges.

Two more explanations for Wilson Hall spirits deal with the overabundance of cemeteries in Athens. The first suggests that when you draw the graveyard pentagram, Wilson is dead center, so to speak. Another theory suggests that Wilson Hall was built on top of a sacred Native American burial ground.

There's very little evidence of the sacred site and, since the pentagram can be drawn in any number of ways, connecting any number of cemeteries, there are doubters of that explanation, too.

Some intrepid students have sought to find the solution to our question of what haunts Wilson by themselves. One student and former Wilson Hall resident, Drew Tonkovich, told the student newspaper that they used a Ouija board to contact the spirits—and there are a few.

One spirit said her name was "Sarah." Sarah then filled the students in with a little background information. She was 69 and died in 1864. Another group of students borrowed the Ouija board and got the same info!

However, another spirit came through when the students ventured into the boiler room. The board spelled out L-U-C-I-F-E-R. Tonkovich said the board was "properly" disposed of after this incident.

The most convincing encounter with a spirit at Wilson Hall comes from R. J. Abraham. He's an Athens native, a former educator, and local historian who is an expert on the Ohio University hauntings. He was the guide for the Fox Television crew when they came to explore Wilson.

According to Abraham, he had his own encounter with the ghost of a young girl when he was trying to find the haunted room.

"I swear I saw a spirit that looked like the girl from *The Shining*, the movie, in the bathroom, and she was pointing. When I followed her finger, I found the supposedly haunted room we had been searching for."

So, if you've been counting the explanations for why Wilson Hall is so haunted, the answer to the question appears to be "e," all of the above.

## The Main Building—University of Notre Dame
### *The Founder's Spirit Lives On, Wanders On*

At 187-feet tall and crowned with a recently regilded gold dome, the Main Building is the second tallest building on campus (after the Basilica of the Sacred Heart). On top of the dome, a 19-foot tall, two ton statue of Mary, the Mother of God, serenely watches over the beloved campus.

It's one of the most recognized buildings on campus. If stories are correct, the Main Building carries on the Notre Dame tradition as an open campus for spirits and ghosts.

There are a few spirits said to be lurking in the Main Building, which now serves primarily as home to the administrative offices of Notre Dame. Perhaps the most famous ghost in the building is Father Sorin, the founder of Notre Dame.

Sorin was a French priest sent as a missionary to the hinterlands of America in the mid-1800s. He became a passionate and prolific founder of institutions of higher learning. Not only did he found Notre Dame, but he also founded St. Edwards University in Austin, Texas.

He was a roving type of guy—and so is his spirit.

Not only has Father Sorin's spirit been seen in the Main Building, but he appeared to pack up with his fellow administrators when they relocated during the Main Building's restoration project. During the construction project, the administrators and staff were moved to Hayes-Healy Hall, according to Father Robert Austgen, who collects campus ghost stories.

As the group settled into their new digs, strange things began to happen.

In one incident, a group of cleaning staff members reported seeing a priest "with a long habit" who was walking through the corridors.

Let's face it, seeing a priest at Notre Dame isn't exactly a reason to call in, well, a priest for an exorcism. There are priests all over campus. But, when the staff looked closely at this particular religious figure, one worker noted that he didn't have any feet.

Oh, and, he glided through a wall!

Father Sorin has actually been seen all over campus. It seems that even after all this time, the good father can't bear the thought of departing from his cherished campuses.

# 4

# HAUNTED LIBRARIES

It's no wonder that libraries rank high on the list of haunted buildings at colleges and universities.

There's a sense of solemnity and seriousness in a library that you often don't feel anywhere else on campus.

Libraries also are intimately connected with the past. Stand in the middle of a stack of books and imagine all the people, many long-deceased, who wrote these books. You are surrounded by their voices, if you just listen.

Campus libraries are haunted by dozens of different types of spirits—from interactive ghosts to poltergeists.

Active spirits seem to play a prominent role in library hauntings. Students and staff alike claim to see apparitions darting through the rows of books. The apparitions vary in size and appearance—some are filmy and shapeless, while others are so real you could almost reach out and touch them—although that wouldn't be recommended.

Class clowns and pranksters aren't the only ones who find plenty of opportunities for mischief at the library. Poltergeists—our pranksters from the other side—have been known to slam a few doors and send a few books flying down the aisle.

The sources of these types of hauntings can be just as varied as the manifestations. Former librarians are a frequent scapegoat for paranormal activity, but famous university founders and figures get their share of the blame, too.

Students, usually the victim of a tragic incident or accident, can haunt libraries, too.

We'll start our tour at one of the most famous haunted libraries in the South—and maybe in the U.S. Gorgas Library at the University of Alabama is one of those spots where ghosts check in, but they never check out.

## Gorgas House and Gorgas Library— University of Alabama

### *The Gorgas Family Ghosts*

The Gorgas family gave a lot to the University of Alabama.

Josiah Gorgas, a former Confederate general, and his wife, Amelia Gayle, helped shepherd the school through the uncertain days immediately following the Civil War. Josiah served as president until illness forced him to retire. Amelia Gayle served as the school librarian, nurse, friend to homesick cadets, hostess, and pretty much anything else the university asked the daughter of the former Alabama governor to be.

But that's not all the Gorgas family gave the University of Alabama. The family bequeathed dozens of ghost stories to its students. In fact, almost every place that's labeled with the name, "Gorgas," is haunted.

Josiah and Amelia Gayle once lived in the quaint Gorgas House, which now serves as a university museum that displays antiques and Gorgas family items. At times, the home features a display of a supernatural sort. The ghost of a solider—some suspect Josiah, himself—has been seen and heard walking the halls of Gorgas House. In the creepiest reports, witnesses report hearing the banging of a sword against the wall as the ghost moves through the home.

A university is only as good as its library. And a library is only as good as its ghosts.

Gorgas Library has a wide selection of ghosts. The spectral suspects include Amelia Gayle, herself.

When she served as librarian, Amelia Gayle was completely dedicated to creating the best university library in the south. She added new books to the collection, a collection that was all but destroyed by Yankee soldiers.

Paranormal researchers say that the librarian's love and dedication for the university and its students may be the reason that Amelia Gayle may have never left the position as university librarian. Strange activity continues to this day. One strange reminder is the elevator's peculiar behavior. Workers and students say that the elevator stops off on the fourth floor even though they didn't request the stop. Likewise, employees on the fourth floor say they've watched the elevator stop and the door glide open. They're shocked when they see that no one is in the elevator car. It's empty. Or is the spirit of Amelia Gayle just making a visit to her namesake library?

Some chat on Facebook adds more details to the stories of Alabama's haunted library. Students report seeing an apparition of a woman who looked a lot like Amelia Gayle.

They've also heard someone call their name.

"Apparently one of the girls who worked at the music library last year kept hearing a sound like someone calling her name while she was shelf reading, thought it was her imagination, stopped to listen, and promptly heard someone call her name. Needless to say, she got out of there pretty quick."

Just like shadows chase light, stories of ghosts and spirits tag right behind tales of violence and destruction.

## Hoskins Library—University of Tennessee
### *Evening Primrose and Haunted Hoskins*

Quiet as a tomb.

Alone.

Stoic.

Walking through the campus library, especially during off-peak hours, can make you feel like *you* are the ghost. And, when you can't find the book you're looking for in the stacks and stacks of volumes, you understand why ghosts seem to wander aimlessly through certain campus buildings.

You could probably ask the staff and students at Hoskins Library at the University of Tennessee what it feels like to haunt—and be haunted—at the campus library.

You might start your inquiry by talking to someone like John. They refer to John as a maintenance specialist at Hoskins Library, which resembles a medieval fortress, but he was more like a guard—a guard on watch for supernatural outbreaks in the library.

As he made his rounds at the library over the years, John said he heard, saw, felt, and even smelled weird things.

He told the student newspaper that on a few occasions, usually during odd power outages at the building; he had a few run-ins with the paranormal. Once, he heard someone walking through the library and even heard doors close. Another time, he felt a presence—even though there was no one near him.

More ominously, John claimed to hear the rattling of chains and the sound of heavy breathing.

Then, there are the out-of-place smells. He told the newspaper:

"Sometimes you can smell cornbread and beef stew cooking, (but) there are no kitchens in the place. There have been people through the years who've said they've seen her on the staircases and things like that. I've never seen her personally."

Most students believe John's accounts are proof positive that the spirit that they call, "Evening Primrose" is haunting Hoskins.

Evening Primrose—the story goes—was a graduate student who was working on her doctoral dissertation. She stationed herself in the library and began the tedious chore of research for her paper. Some say she avoided food, others say the strain of the dissertation process was too much for her. Whatever the cause, Evening Primrose died in the library. They found her under a stack of books.

Evening Primrose would never get that doctorate. She would be forced to wander the halls of Hoskins, forever ABD—all but dissertation.

On the other hand, maybe ABD stands for Anything But Dead.

Nonetheless, Evening Primrose continues her research work.

## Pattee Library—Penn State

*Overdue Spirits*

Not all the spirits of Penn State seem as content in the afterworld as Old Coaly, the ghost of a mule who just enjoys a stroll around the campus in the dark of night.

Some spirits seem to be trying to express their unhappiness of being taken out of the world of the living so soon.

One of the most disturbing Big Ten ghost stories is the tale of the murdered coed and a restless spirit that continues to search through the rows of bookshelves in Penn State's main library, Pattee Library.

It's not just Penn State students who feel that there's just something different about the library. Alumni, guests, and even high school students from the nearby town of State College travel to the library to check out the extensive book collection, peruse magazines and newspapers from all over the world, and conduct research.

For one high school student, her research at Pattee took a frightening, paranormal turn. The unnamed witness told a local magazine that she was in the library one evening. Even though she was probably not the only person in Pattee at the time, the unique interior layout of the building made it seem like she was all alone. Students have dubbed the labyrinth of shelves "the stacks." The rows are barely wide enough to compensate for the extra "Freshman 15"—the sudden weight gain students say they experience in that nerve-racking first year.

The witness said she was wandering alone when she saw a young lady who seemed to be wandering through the stacks, too. That in itself, didn't faze her. But the witness said there was something strange about the lady, a feeling or aura, perhaps. Then, the schoolgirl saw that the clothes of the student seemed to be from a different time period.

As her eyes traveled down the body of the student, she noticed that her feet did not quite touch the ground.

It was a full-bodied apparition.

Students and those who are familiar with the Pattee Library haunting speculate that this high school student may have had a rare, first-person encounter with the spirit of a murdered female student.

Late one November afternoon in 1969, police say an anguished cry cut through the stacks, a cry that still reverberates. A fellow student heard that scream and rushed to find the source. There, in one of the oldest sections of the stacks, the student discovered Betsy Aardsma, the victim of a brutal stabbing.

While many students deserted the campus during the long Thanksgiving weekend, Betsy, a pretty English graduate student, stayed behind.

Betsy was taken for medical attention at the Ritenour Building, the student health center, but it was too late. She died as a result of her wounds.

The murder was never solved.

It's easy for students to connect this tragic event with the occasional report of an actual apparition, like the one we discussed earlier. But spirits manifest in other, more subtle ways. There are reports that the cool draft blowing through the stacks is a reminder that the library is never actually deserted.

Witnesses have reported that they often feel an odd, eerie presence when they're walking alone in the stacks. Those who have experienced the phenomena say they feel like they're being watched. These claims don't just come from students, even library workers report the strange phenomena, saying that the presence is most keenly felt in the top section of Pattee.

There are also stories of a sudden breeze cropping up from an inexplicable origin. After all, if a person can barely fit through the stacks, surely wind would be blocked.

Several witnesses have even heard an anguished cry while studying in the stacks.

Is it the echo of Betsy Aardsma's chilling scream or a cry of a ghost hoping for justice?

Or maybe just a shriek of student who's had one term paper too many?

## Memorial Library—University of Wisconsin
*Some Spirits Never Check Out*

The librarians at Memorial Library at the University of Wisconsin can always keep the students quiet, but they have a hard time shushing the spirit activity among the stacks of books and long, solemn study rooms.

Memorial Library at the University of Wisconsin is reportedly haunted by a few spirits, including one who would have no trouble with stories and tales. Helen Constance White, a novelist and professor who died in 1967, was known not only for her powerful teaching style and intensity as a writer, but also for her purple wardrobe.

She was also remembered with her catch phrase.

White would often tell a departing student or colleague, "I hope our paths will cross again."

Even though White is the one who has departed, she still crosses paths with students every now and then. She has been seen standing in the stacks of the library and is said to roam the halls of the library, still looking for a good read.

She may have crossed paths in the spirit world with another university library ghost: Sally Brown.

Students and librarians say that they have heard someone—or something—whisper "Sally Brown" in their ears. According to some reports, Sally Brown haunts the Memorial Library; others say she hung out in, or at least floated around, the library.

Who Sally Brown actually is and what library she actually haunts is a matter of some debate on campus, but at least she uses proper library etiquette and whispers her name.

## Blegen Library—University of Cincinnati
### *Rare Books, Typical Spooks*
As a library goes, the exterior of the Blegen Library at the University of Cincinnati is pretty common for a decades-old campus library. A stoic façade and understated landscaping reflect the scholarly, serious work that goes on inside the library

At Blegen, there's a lot to read—even on the outside. Two inscriptions are etched into the walls of the library. This first is from Sir Francis Bacon, "Read not to contradict and confute, nor to believe and take for granted, nor to talk and discourse, but to weigh and consider."

John Milton adds the second inscription, which has a paranormal twist, "For books are not absolutely dead things but do contain a potencie on life in them to be as active as he whose progeny they are."

Hmmm…Good to know.

The outside of Blegen is normal—serious, but normal. When you step inside, though, things begin to get seriously spooky. Students will tell you the whole library may be haunted, but to get the full effect of the Blegen haunting, you have to go to the rare-book stacks on the ninth floor, named for, by the way, one of America's great classic literature scholars, Carl Blegen. A prodigious collector of ancient Greek works, Blegen would love the rare-books section of his namesake library. The section is surrounded by walls of rare books. But, of course, maybe I'm not telling Blegen anything new; his spirit is one of the suspects that students say is haunting this section.

According to students and staff, an apparition of a man has appeared in the library. He's about 5-foot-8 and looks to be in his forties. The ghost, who sports a tweed jacket and cap, also has a professorial air about him.

He's quick for a dead guy, too. One university archivist, who echoes a lot of reported supernatural incidents in the library, said that a feeling that someone is watching you is the first sign that the Blegen Library ghost is present. But when you look around, the ghost is nowhere to be found.

Only a few lucky—or unlucky, depending on your take on haunted activities—have caught sight of the ghost.

There are other signs that something paranormal is checking in at the library. People hear books moving around. Sometimes people report the sound of footsteps and sense a cold wind, like someone is passing by.

Kevin Grace, the university archivist, puts it politically, "When you're up there working by yourself, it's very easy to think that somebody's watching you."

Archivists also claim they're certain they put a book back in its proper place, only to find it in a completely different area. (And archivists don't tend to be the practical joking types.)

It's easy to see why almost everyone thinks Blegen is haunted, though. It's intentionally kept chilly. Paranormal researchers say that the temperature drops before a ghost appears, so it may always seem like an apparition might pop up at Blegen. Also, the stacks are crammed with old books. And when we say old, we're talking about manuscripts from as far back as the 1500s with gold gilt. Students say that maybe one of the owners of these old books came along for the spirit ride to the library.

Another theory: There is a whole field of paranormal research that deals with haunted objects—voodoo dolls and bad-luck charms. Did Carl Blegen bring back some cursed book during one of his book-finding trips to Greece? (Although a lot of students think all of classic literature is cursed when they're assigned to read the heavy tomes.)

Finally, others speculate that the ghost is of a popular Cincy classics professor who spent a lot of time in Blegen. When he died—a little early—he came back to the place he thought of as his home away from home, the library.

Or, could there be a far more natural explanation? The rare-books section is intentionally kept cool, dark, and quiet. Little sounds seem amplified. Shadows consume the light. Skeptics say it's just this type of environment that allows the human imagination to run full tilt.

We may never know the answer. University officials have declined the frequent requests from ghostbusters and paranormal research groups to conduct an investigation at the library. It's just not the place for this type of frivolous activity.

Or could it be that they know there are more things than just old books hiding in the stacks of the Blegen Library?

# 5

# HAUNTED QUADS, GROUNDS, AND CEMETERIES

## A Walk on the Wild Side

We can all agree that the most likely place to find a ghost on campus would be in one of the buildings. It's pretty easy imagining some spirit hanging out in the old dorm that's tucked away in the nether reaches of the campus. And it's not a stretch to think that one of the first places built on campus might have a few haunted tales attached.

But could the very ground where a university is situated be haunted? Could ghosts prowl the lawns, yards, and forests of a school and duck into buildings that are constructed around this hallowed—or haunted —ground?

Paranormal researchers and folklorists both respond to these questions with a resounding "Yes!"

Quads, which are typically spacious, green areas bordered by buildings and serve as a focal point for campuses, can be just as haunted as old administration buildings and libraries. This is most true in the South where a few schools had their quads turned into Civil War battlefields and medical stations for the injured and dying. Spirits of those soldiers remain on campuses like the University of Alabama and the University of Tennessee.

In some cases, universities suffer from ill-advised placement. For example, some campuses were constructed on ground already considered sacred by Native Americans.

And the ghosts of cemeteries placed on campus? Well, that goes without saying.

There are even those who suggest that the haunted buildings on campus are paranormally active because the ground, itself, is haunted. Ghosts drift off of the quad and into the buildings, this theory states.

Our first stop is at the University of Alabama, where Sherman has left his mark on more than burned-buildings on campus; he has left wandering souls who still make their presence known to staff, faculty, students, and visitors.

## The Haunted Quad—University of Alabama
### *The South Shall Rise (from the Dead) Again*

The University of Alabama has at least one thing in common with many other schools in the SEC (Southeastern Conference) and with schools in the South, in general—lots of ghosts.

Though it happened well over a hundred years ago, the spirits of the men who fought in the Civil War just can't seem to let go of the land they fought—and died—for.

The university is particularly vulnerable to these military spirits. The university once served as a military academy, and many of the soldiers that donned gray for the Southern cause were trained on the fields and in the buildings of the grounds that have since become the University of Alabama. They marched and maneuvered right on the Quad before shipping off to the battle between the states, a little war that every Southern boy knew would only last six months. Then they'd be right back on the ol' Quad.

But months stretched into years. And many of these men never made it back home to their beloved Quad. If student legends are correct, maybe their physical bodies didn't return to the Quad, but their spirits managed to return.

The cadets of the University of Alabama didn't have to go far to earn their piece of immortality. It came looking for them. When the Union entered Tuscaloosa, the commandant of the academy, Col. James T. Murfree, ordered the cadets to make a stand against the invaders.

They mustered near Gorgas Library and marched to the fight.

Hopelessly outnumbered and vastly undersupplied, the brave cadets, nonetheless, marched out to face the best the Union could hand them. They soon found out.

After forming a defensive line, the cadets waited for their adversaries to come in range of their antiquated Springfield rifles. A withering volley tore into the Union ranks. The Yankees, perhaps a bit surprised by the ferocity of the attack from a bunch of kids, reeled. But not for long.

The Union counterattacked and the superior forces forced the cadets who weren't struck down to withdraw back to the university.

Since then, dozens of reports of strange happenings on the Quad and in buildings near the Quad have filtered through the student body over the years. One common tale is that four Civil War soldiers wander the grounds at night. Often, the witness can make out the uniforms of the martial ghosts. Speculation is it's the cadets preparing for one more go at the damn Yankees.

Oddly, one ghost of the Quad isn't a Southern boy or an Alabama cadet. He's a Yankee. According to this legend, once the Union troops had fully possessed Tuscaloosa and the cadets were routed, a soldier was ordered to enter the campus and meet with the cadets of the military academy. The end of the war was near, but passions still flamed. The Union emissary was killed. Some say he was murdered in the octagonal-shaped Little Round House, originally used as a guard house. Now, if you pass by the Little Round House, or, heaven forbid, are actually in the Little Round House at night, you might hear the sound of someone rummaging through the rooms. People have heard footsteps, the sound of furniture moving, and even the clank of whiskey bottles echoing from the building, which is now used as a memorial for honor societies.

Ironically, the Little Round House escaped total destruction when flames ignited by Union soldiers destroyed the rest of campus. What protected the site? How did it escape the all-encompassing flames? The answer, paranormal experts say, is easy—spirits.

## The Haunted Hill—University of Tennessee
### *How Hallowed Ground Becomes Haunted Ground*

The University of Tennessee, like most universities, contains sacred ground, areas where students gather or celebrate. There are also sacred places where founders and officials have designated as areas to hold university functions.

But the University of Tennessee didn't need to have sacred ground appointed by rowdy students or the founding fathers. The American Civil War saw to that.

The University of Tennessee's campus is near a piece of ground that was once the scene of a violent battle between Union and Confederate armies, called the Battle of Fort Sanders.

On November 29, 1863, a large group of Confederate troops commanded by Lt. Gen. James Longstreet attacked a vastly outnumbered band of Union soldiers stationed in a bastion named Fort Sanders. For

Longstreet, a military genius who was commanding an overwhelming force, the fort looked vulnerable.

He was wrong.

Within 20 minutes, Longstreet's attack turned into a disaster. A line of his troops were caught up in a tangle of telegraph wire as they struggled up the hill. The attack faltered and then the soldiers retreated back down the hill. A bulk of the forces fell into a trench and were picked off by the few hundred Union troops. A new invention—the hand grenade—was used to finish off the remaining soldiers caught in the death trap.

The Confederates retreated from Knoxville. The Union soldiers buried their dead.

But some say the spirits of the soldiers live on.

Ghosts of the Civil War heroes are among the spirits said to wander the University of Tennessee's sacred spot, now just referred to as The Hill. Whether it's fate—or poor paranormal planning—a number of dormitories are among the buildings situated on this sacred ground. If there's one thing that doesn't mix, it's haunted ground and dorms.

Over the years, students in these dormitories have reported strange noises and even an apparition or two.

The official Tennessee website admits to a few sightings. In the lawn next to Perkins Hall, witnesses have watched as a group of eight Union soldiers confer over a map. The conditions to see these soldiers must be exactly right. Legend has it that they appear during clear nights with plenty of moonlight to help illuminate their map.

Before the map-reading ghosts were reported, most of the Civil War hauntings occurred at Blount Hall, a dorm that was razed in 1979.

A female student residing in Blount Hall said she was sleeping soundly one night when she jolted awake. She said she had the feeling that somebody was watching her.

She probably didn't want to look, but eventually she looked at the foot of her bed and saw a man. The student described him as a tall, gaunt figure clad in a Civil War-era uniform. His eyes glowed, she said. The girl screamed and the ghost faded away.

Cynics say it was a prank. But male students at the time said it was easier to crack a safe in Fort Knox than enter the girls' dorm after hours. Security was legendary.

Homeowners who live in the neighborhood near The Hill add to the mystery. They say that they've seen figures gliding eerily across the lawn of the Hill. Witnesses say they can make out the gray and blue uniforms among the specters.

It's not just military ghosts who guard The Hill. Tales of a massive black dog have circulated through the student body. Experts on folklore call this dog a barghest. Tales of barghests appear to come from northern England, especially in the Yorkshire area.

In Tennessee, the black dog guards The Hill, its eyes glowing red and saliva dripping from its fangs.

Vicious barks and yelps have stirred students who live in the nearby dorms from their sleep on more than one occasion.

Not all Tennessee students believe the dog is a barghest, or any other mythical creature. This camp insists that the dog is the ghost of Bonita, the pet of the Tyson family. Bonita rests under a small gravestone on the grounds of the Tyson House. Bonita was a gift from Ulysses Simpson Grant, Jr., the son of the famous Civil War general and U.S. president, to the family's daughter. She might also be the source of the Tyson House haunting, as well as the barghest who searches the Hill for its long-gone master and mistress.

The Tennessee campus is particularly vulnerable to hauntings. The scene of a battle and resting place for mythological creatures have made the university a hot spot for hauntings. What more could they do to attract spirits? How about building near a Native American graveyard? That should do it.

# Agricultural Campus—University of Tennessee

*Ancient Spirits and Campus Founders Wander the Ag Campus*

The University of Tennessee could make a run for, if not a national title, then at least an conference title for the most haunted campus. With ghost dogs and haunted mansions, the university's ghosts blanket the campus.

You would think that the calm, pristine lands of the school's Agricultural Campus, which lies adjacent to the main Knoxville campus, would be spirit free.

But you'd be wrong.

Dead wrong.

The land that now serves as one of the premier agricultural research centers is also home to a Hamilton-era burial mound. The burial mound is said to contain the graves of between 10 and 100 American Indians. The burial site is probably more than a thousand years old. Its exact location is considered restricted.

But stories about the ghosts of Native Americans aren't restricted to this burial site. Paranormal research experts guess that the proximity of the gravesite to the campus could be one reason for the spirit activity on the grounds and in several buildings in the area referred to as the Agricultural Campus.

Morgan Hall is located near the site. Perhaps it's close enough to pick up some occult activity. Over the years, like the mist that settles on the campus, several reports about hauntings and ghostly encounters have drifted in.

One member of the staff said he's witnessed some weird happenings at Morgan Hall, a Gothic-style building that was the headquarters of the Institute of Agriculture.

Charles Walker was working as an Ag journalist in the building. He was working late one night—that's how a lot of these stories start—then he saw something. Here's how he tells the story to student journalist:

"…and I was madly typing away, and out of the corner of my eye, I saw a man standing in black by the cabinets out in front of my office.

I jumped so hard that my knees hit the keyboard, and needless to say, I spun around in that direction…

"…and there was nothing there."

The description certainly didn't sound like a Native American, but Walker's sighting did confirm a legend that the ghost wears clothes from an earlier era. He's also been known to top off his ensemble with a derby hat. There are a few guesses who Morgan Hall's man-in-black is. He's rumored to be the ghost of a gentleman who died while working in the building. But no one's sure.

## The Main Quadrangle—University of Illinois
### *A So-Called Solemn Spot with Its Share of Paranormal Activity*

Like a lot of university campuses, the University of Illinois has a quad. The Quad is a grassy nook surrounded by the school's main buildings that's designed for relaxing and—less frequently—for studying.

The Main Quadrangle at University of Illinois starts at the new Main University Hall to the north and runs to the Auditorium to the south.

Among these buildings, in between Altgeld Hall and Henry Administration Building, stands a peculiar monument. It's a simple stone that marks the gravesite of the college's founding president, John Milton Gregory.

Gregory was the university's first president and arguably its most important. He was instrumental in merging classical liberal education with industrial and agriculture lessons.

While students and faculty have a chance to relax on the Quad, the busy President Gregory, apparently, does not have a chance to kick back and read a good book. Gregory's spirit is just one of the apparitions to make a regular appearance on the school's haunted Quad. Students have reported seeing a forlorn presence on the campus from time to time, strolling through the grounds.

Witnesses say that the presence doesn't look like a professor or student, at least not living ones. It's a filmy, waving presence moving across the Quad, a presence that they say resembles the old pictures of President Gregory.

And there's something strange about the inscription on Gregory's simple grave. It says, "if you seek his monument, look about you." Most say that this little summation means that the entire university serves as a monument for Gregory's leadership and hard work establishing one of the nation's preeminent places of learning.

But others—particularly students with a more supernatural bent—say that the saying means that President Gregory continues to make his presence known on the Quad. "Look about you," the students say, "and you'll see him."

It's not just the Quad that is reportedly haunted at the University of Illinois; it's merely the epicenter. In fact, most of the buildings around the Quad have a ghost story or urban legend attached to them, including the aforementioned Altgeld Hall, home of the university's Mathematics Department.

The mathematics building's peculiar Romanesque architecture has drawn rumors that students are doing more than computing—they're communing with the spirit world. First of all, believers say the building has 33 levels. Architect and Illinois professor Nathan Clifford Ricker considered 33 an auspicious number for some reason. To get the desired number of levels, the Altgeld seems to have incorporated stairways that lead to nowhere in its original design when it was built as Library Hall back in 1896.

Some students say these stairways connect to other of Ricker-designed buildings like some type of three-dimensional, metaphysical jigsaw puzzle. Ricker also designed the Drill Hall (later named Kenney Gym Annex), the Natural History Building, and the Metal Shop, which was razed in 1993, just to name a few.

Not all agree.

According to skeptics, the building doesn't have 33 levels and all the stairways don't form some type of architectural jigsaw puzzle. One more thing these skeptics add: it's not a portal to anywhere. Well, maybe—the Altgeld is a portal to a degree in mathematics.

Obviously, it's a debate that still simmers on the campus of the University of Illinois. But at least when it comes to the supernatural, the haunted Quad has lots of places to debate.

## Eugene Pioneer Cemetery—University of Oregon
### *Ghost Hunting 101: The Ultimate Final Exam*

Surrounded on three sides, Eugene Pioneer Cemetery juts into the heart of the University of Oregon's campus. It's one of the oldest cemeteries in Eugene and definitely the largest. Stretching over 16 acres, the cemetery contains about 5,000 burials.

That's a lot of potential ghost stories.

The coexistence between the living and the dead has not always been a peaceful one. Over the years, several bills were introduced at the state legislature to have the property condemned and the graves removed to make way for an expanded campus. Those initiatives died in committee. No pun intended.

From what we've learned in this book about the paranormal ramifications for disturbing graves, the students should be glad that the legislation failed. The paranormal forces that such a move would have unleashed on the campus are easy to imagine.

A spiritual truce has since existed. While most people would suspect that the cemetery would be the victim of vandalism because it is so close to campus, authorities say that it's not the case. Besides some well-trod paths cut through the cemetery as shortcuts to campus and a few Frisbee matches, the students treat the cemetery with extreme respect.

The students seem to even enjoy the peace of the little plot of ground as a spot of meditation and quiet.

But they also know the cemetery is haunted.

Each fall, right around Halloween, students gather for a little ghost-busting session. It's become an annual tradition.

In 2009, leaders of the Pacific Paranormal Research Society conducted the Ghost Hunting 101 class in the Pioneer Cemetery. That year, the paranormal experts who have conducted more than 100 investigations over 10 years said the students gathered lots of evidence. In fact, they got more evidence than they bargained for.

As the team of about 300 newly trained ghost hunters hit the cemetery, the evidence began to mount. Several investigators outfitted with electromagnetic field detection equipment immediately began to register hits. Another group of investigators were continually snapping pictures, hoping to capture images of orbs or misty spirit forms. A student spirit photographer took one picture with a smoky image. The lead investigator immediately identified it as ectoplasm, a Holy Grail of spiritualists who recognized ectoplasm as a residue left over from a spirit.

Todd Baker, one of the ghost hunting guides said, "He got something real. For a first-time investigator, that's a really big deal."

# 6

# THEATERS, MUSIC BUILDINGS, AND PERFORMANCE HALLS

## The Ghosts Must Go On

The theater is a place where people go to willingly allow their belief to be suspended. They have no trouble believing that the sophomore on stage is a 60-year-old traveling salesman. Or that it's quite natural to break out into a song while taking a buggy ride through Oklahoma.

Is this willing suspension of belief why campus theaters and music halls are so haunted?

That's only one theory.

Students who have had spirit encounters in theaters have another theory, though. This theory states that theaters are haunted because they have so many friggin' ghosts in them.

## Gallaway Theatre—University of Alabama

### *The Haunting Must Go On*

Gallaway Theatre, located in Rowand-Johnson Hall, has seen its share of drama over the years, some of which, was actually onstage.

Not to discount the fine work of the university's fine actors and actresses, but there's another storyline that connects the current drama students with the past. Marian Gallaway, who lends her name to the theater and was the university's theater director from 1948 to 1973, reportedly has never exited stage right—or stage left.

Lots of theater students have seen and felt the presence of Marian in the Gallaway.

One student, on his first day of class, said he walked past a lady on the way to class. He said hello to the lady, who seemed to acknowledge his presence.

While it was a typical encounter, there was something strange about the greeting. He just couldn't put his finger on it.

He entered the theater and met a few of his fellow students. That's when he noticed a painting on the wall. It obviously portrayed the woman he just said hello to.

"I just saw this lady," the new student said. "I saw her right outside."

There was a silent stretch as the other actors and actresses looked at each other. They then announced., "Well, if you did, you saw the ghost of Marian Gallaway. She's been dead for several years now."

The group, no doubt, filled him in on some other ghostly tales of the former theater director.

There's one legend that death may keep Marian off the mortal coil, but it hasn't kept her from offering direction to her charges. Reportedly, if a student says, "How's my blocking, Mrs. Gallaway," the spirit of the theater director will appear in the projection booth at the rear of the theater.

Even Tennessee Williams has a part of the hauntings at the university. Marian Gallaway, the theater director during the mid-twentieth century, has appeared dressed in white on the stage in her theater in Rowand-Johnson Hall. Marian's husband had left her to pursue a romance with Tennessee Williams, and Williams supposedly used Marian as the inspiration for Blanche DuBois in *A Streetcar Named Desire*.

## E.C. Mabie Theatre—University of Iowa
### *Death Doesn't Stop "the Boss"*

Most people who walk through E. C. Mabie Theatre on the University of Iowa campus swear they're not the audience anymore; they feel like they're part of a show—and someone is watching them.

It might be the strange, ever-watchful eyes on the painting of the one-time theater legend that gives these visitors the creeps.

In his day, E. C. (Edward Charles) Mabie, who is portrayed in the painting, was one of the most well-known professors on the University of Iowa campus. He was an academic rock star, but formidable was the word more often used to describe him. His students, like Tennessee Williams, had other terms they used to describe their instructor. They were writers after all.

One of those nicknames was "Boss." His most famous student had a run-in with Boss Mabie. The story, which appeared in *Tom...The Unknown Tennessee Williams* by Lyle Leverich, covers Mabie's reaction to an assignment that Williams turned in one day. Williams wrote a play that appeared to endorse socialized medicine. Mabie went ballistic and tore up the script. Mabie apparently had a few friends who were doctors and found Williams's play insulting.

Despite the volatility, Mabie is credited with turning the Department of Speech and Dramatic Art from one mainly concerned with public speaking into a highly regarded theatrical arts department.

Students and fellow professors all agree: Mabie had a strong spirit. Still does, as a matter of fact.

If you believe the stories passed on by students, staff, and faculty, Professor Mabie still has tenure at the university theater. He occasionally drops by to make sure his students are still writing, acting, and directing to his high standards. Theater students say that the spirit of E. C. Mabie has been seen watching performances. More than one student has noticed a strange figure—a guy who looks oddly out of place—sitting in the audience. They say this odd audience member, dressed in clothes of a bygone era, bears an unmistakable resemblance to the portrait of E. C. Mabie that hangs in the lobby.

Other witnesses say Mabie isn't just taking in the show for the fun of it; he's critiquing the performance. And, if the severe look on his face is any indication, E. C. Mabie has not let death take anything away from his formidable reputation as a theater critic.

Judith Moessner, a staff member in the division of Performing Arts at the time of her interview, reported that there are stories that the strange audience member can be heard mumbling his criticisms and clicking his tongue in disgust at times.

But his presence isn't just felt at performances and rehearsals. Like all great lovers of the theater, Mabie's ghost is at the theater at all hours and in all places. He lives and breathes theater. Well, he breathes it, at least. Once, when the marketing office was housed a floor below the audience seating section, a former marketing director said he heard the distinct sound of footsteps echoing overhead. It sounded like someone walking to their seat—even though the director knew there was no one else in the theater.

Was it E. C. preparing for his latest harsh review? We may never know. The director never reported whether he went to investigate.

In 2008, a flood damaged the theater. The costume shop—perhaps the most haunted section of the theater—was particularly hard hit. And the spirits were not happy. A group of students who volunteered to help clean out and repair the costume shop and nearby offices said they saw a strange shadow linger in the area.

Just as suddenly, the shadow vanished.

It turns out that Mabie also seems particularly attached to his portrait that hangs in the theater lobby. If the portrait is moved or, God forbid, taken down, trouble ensues. On a few occasions, the portrait has been removed or taken down temporarily, workers say that furniture is moved. Then, there are those anomalous events—stage lights exploding, unlocked doors locking, etc.—that students don't write off as mere bad luck. They think it's a message from E. C. And the portrait gets re-hung quickly.

Other paranormal events at the theater include a shadowy figure seen in the basement. The figure is seen near where the costume shop was originally situated.

Mabie, by the way, doesn't just haunt the theater. Evidence suggests his presence continued to haunt some of his most famous student's work long after graduation, or after he drummed them out of the university. Williams, for example, used the Mabie surname in a play fragment "Death: Celebration." Mabie would have probably appreciated the irony.

## Northrop Auditorium—University of Minnesota
### *Ghost Ex Machina*

Cyrus Northrop Memorial Auditorium, named after the University of Minnesota's second president, is the scene of some great theatrical spectacles. Not all of these spectacles are plays, concerts, or dance recitals. According to theater students and staff, the theater is haunted.

The building, which was constructed in 1929, seats more than 4,000 people and at least one ghost.

According to an article in the school newspaper, the *Minnesota Daily*, a former stage manager has never left the theater. The manager, reportedly an alcoholic who basically lived in the theater, began work when the auditorium was built and continued to work there until he died in the 1960s.

"Scores of stories" have been circulated about the manager with many of the eyewitness accounts placing the ghost in the balcony or on the stage.

The ghost of Northrop Auditorium has appeared as a full-body apparition of a man working on stage. As the name suggests, a full-body apparition is a complete manifestation of a ghost, although these apparitions often appear "filmy" or transparent. It's also one of the rarest manifestations of the paranormal and makes this haunting particularly interesting for ghost hunters and paranormal investigators.

Ushers and staff members seem to have the most run-ins with the ghost of Northrop. According to a story that appeared in a 2002 student-newspaper article, two stage workers were at the auditorium one night. While working in the sound booth at the rear of the auditorium, one worker heard the door bang repeatedly.

Naturally, he assumed his coworker was making the racket, but when he got near the door, nobody was there. At that instant, he spied his coworker across the auditorium. He realized that the coworker could not have banged the door and made it across the auditorium in the mere seconds that elapsed.

Footsteps are another reminder that someone is still waiting for an encore long after the crowds have gone home. One former student and worker reported hearing the rhythmic pattern of footsteps above the break room and above the stage manager's office, even though no one else was supposed to be in that area of the building.

Despite his reputation as a surly alcoholic, the presence doesn't seem to be a mean drunk.

"I guess he's just making sure everything is going okay," the auditorium's operations director told the student newspaper.

Northrop isn't the only theater with a paranormal audience member. Schwab Auditorium at Penn State, for example, has a few ghosts who take in plays and musical performances.

# Schwab Auditorium—Penn State
### *"Schwaboo" Takes a Bow*

We've already established that ghost stories spread easily on the campus of universities, especially ones with a long and glorious past, like Penn State.

It doesn't help when you have a grave in the middle of campus, either.

And that's exactly what you'll find smack dab in the middle of the Penn State campus.

The last resting place of George W. Atherton, the university's seventh president and arguably its most important, is in a simple grave on Pollock Road, smack dab in the center of campus. It's a fitting memorial for someone who gave so much to create Penn State. Atherton is credited with restoring the shaky academic and financial fitness of the young university.

But Atherton's legacy is far from dead and buried. Right next to the grave is Schwab Auditorium, reportedly the most haunted building on campus.

Coincidence?

Atherton is just one of the spectral suspects behind some of the creepy theatrics of Schwab Auditorium, a theater that boasts dozens of brilliant actors and musicians, as well as a troupe of ghosts as headliners. The 972-seat auditorium was built between 1902 and 1903 thanks mostly to a contribution given to the university by Charles M. Schwab, a leader in Pennsylvania's booming steel industry and one of the state's richest men, and his wife. The tycoon was also a member of Penn State's board of trustees.

Some say Schwab is the most likely suspect for the bizarre goings-on in the theater.

Whoever or whatever the source, the theater has been the center of numerous paranormal performances.

This is one case of haunting at Penn State that has multiple eyewitness testimonies.

Hagan King, a Penn State student in the early 1970s, is one. He told his story in the September/October 1998 edition of the *Penn Stater* magazine. King said he had the surreal luck to be the last person in Schwab Auditorium one evening in 1970.

King told the *Penn Stater* that he felt like someone was watching him. He looked up at the stage and discovered two figures. The figures seemed to hover above the stage right section and stare at him. One figure appeared to be bigger than the other.

On another occasion, King said he was startled by a noise and saw a shadowy form flutter in and out of a doorway. King also told *Penn Stater* he felt a tug on his arm while he was working offstage. He turned to look, expecting to find someone desiring his attention, but there wasn't anyone next to him, or even close to him.

There are more tales of supernatural drama at the theater. Tom Hesketh was a technical coordinator and production adviser at Schwab. Hesketh said he was working in the attic of the building—identified as a particularly haunted spot by some students and an extremely creepy place by all. He attempted to retrieve a pair of cutters and discovered that they had disappeared, even though he knew he had just laid them down a few seconds before. He checked in his toolbox and then checked out the catwalk After, reluctantly deciding he had simply lost the tool, he locked his toolbox in a cupboard, and left. The next day, he was surprised to find the cutters laying on top of the box, in plain view.

Atherton and Schwab aren't the only spirits who supposedly haunt the theater. According to the *Penn Stater*, two other workers have come forward with their encounters with ghosts in Schwab Auditorium, but their descriptions don't easily fit the typical theories that it's Atherton or Schwab who haunt the theater.

While working at the theater, Peter Zimmerman saw a figure standing in the middle of the stage. At first, Zimmerman thought it was a female coworker. He called out to her, but it wasn't a "her" at all. The shape began—more and more—to take on the appearance of a long-haired man. Zimmerman, his curiosity obviously stoking his courage, drew closer to the figure. After he called out to the man, or whatever it was, the figure glided to the right side of the stage and disappeared right through the solid wall!

Zimmerman's account sounds eerily similar to a story told by another Schwab worker, the general manager of Penn State's Center for Performing Arts, Dave Will. In this case, Will said he was working in the theater late one night in 1972. A figure—cloaked in gray mist—appeared next to him and slowly took the shape of a man clothed in Revolutionary War–era garb. Just like Zimmerman, Will described a man with long hair. The encounter lasted a mere ten seconds, according to Will.

Will explained the phenomena away, telling himself that the man was a figment of his imagination. But after a second encounter with the gray man, his confidence began to fade. In 1977, Will saw the figure again—this time in the basement—and became a believer.

Zimmerman and Will's reports raise some interesting questions. If the building was constructed long after the Revolutionary War, does the haunting predate the auditorium, or even the university? Could a ghost have haunted the woods and fields that became Penn State?

Others have a different theory. Perhaps the long-haired trooper is not a soldier at all, but an actor permanently typecast as a soldier.

Could it be?

On a campus where a mule supposedly haunts a dormitory, an actor haunting an old theater isn't much of a stretch.

# Wisconsin Union Theater —University of Wisconsin
## *Theater Takes Tragedy to New Levels*

The drive to build Wisconsin Union Theater was spearheaded by then-president Charles R. Van Hise. His passion to create the theater was driven by an overwhelming passion—to create the cultural hub for the University of Wisconsin, for its students, and for the residents of Madison. Van Hise pictured the theater drawing acts from all over the world. Its halls, designed with the best acoustical practices in mind, would be filled with music. Its stage would serve as a platform for the best comedies and tragedies ever written.

Some of those tragedies, however, were never written by Shakespeare, Euripides, O'Neill, or any of the other great playwrights; they were conceived by a series of misfortunes that took place in the theater and, if the stories are true, continue to haunt this cultural hub on campus.

The first incident happened during construction. Rumor has it, according to the *Badger Herald*, the student newspaper, that a construction worker died working on the theater in 1939. How he died, or why he died has never been fully explained, although there are dozens of tales that add to the mystery. The mystery only deepened when a percussionist, a timpani player, fell to his death when the percussion section collapsed.

Those two tragic victims have never left the theater, students report. Their spirits are felt and—in rare cases—seen in the building. The ghosts seem more active at night and when students or workers are alone. Some people claim to sense a presence; others see filmy forms walking through the aisles.

Emotions can play tricks on a person and most of the people who witness performances by the theater's veteran paranormal players chalk the experience up to the dark lighting and the somber mood of the place, not to actual ghosts. But they have a harder time explaining some of the other more definite phenomenon. For instance, the lights in the sound booth inexplicably turn on and off by themselves.

Whether Wisconsin Union Theater is blessed with highly emotional spirits, or cursed with real spirits, area ghost hunters aim to find out. The theater is a frequent spot for paranormal investigators. Their conclusion: inconclusive.

But the show will go on.

# McGraw Tower—Cornell University
## *For Whom the Chimes Toll*

Cornell's chimes are an alumni and student favorite.

It's a rare day that the chimes don't peel over the campus. In fact, they usually sound three times a day.

On some Halloweens, the chimes masters offer a special treat. They invite the public to tour the chimes at McGraw Tower. During the Halloween season, the chimes don't play just Cornell favorites and fight songs. You're likely to hear the Addams Family theme or some other creepy tune to celebrate the season.

The tower was the site of another famous paranormal event. Well, abnormal event might be a better description. In October 1997, students and faculty alike gasped when the saw a pumpkin impaled on the spear that crowns the top of McGraw Tower. The gourd became a bit of a campus celebrity, as the university rushed to secure the area to make sure the pumpkin didn't fall off the tower and turn some unwitting pedestrian into a jack-o'-lantern. While university officials worried about safety issues, the student glee club composed a tune about the summa cum laude pumpkin, and students speculated on how the gourd made its way to the top of McGraw.

We can pretty much bet that the great pumpkin phantom probably has nothing to do with the tower's most famous spirit—Jennie McGraw Fiske.

Jennie was the daughter of a lumber millionaire and became the wife of Willard Fiske, a former Cornell librarian. Jennie was stricken with tuberculosis and died as a relatively young lady. The story of her passing is one of the university's more tender tales; a story that may hold the keys to the haunting of McGraw Tower.

According to some university folklorists, Jennie spent a few years traveling throughout Europe while her custom-made mansion was built on Cornell ground. The principal reason for Jennie's European trip was to collect furniture and art for her mansion. But there was another reason. Doctors at the time thought that the Mediterranean climate would help her tuberculosis, especially compared to the chilly air in Ithaca. She stayed in Italy, but the climate worked no wonders on her condition.

Her tuberculosis continued to worsen and Jennie decided to return from her visit to Europe and see her dream mansion.

She was very weak. The coachmen who drove her to the site of the new home said she was able to raise her head and gaze on the mansion. She smiled.

Jennie never lived in the home. She died a few days later. Jennie's interred in Cornell's Sage Chapel.

A Cornell frat bought Jennie's mansion, but the tragedy wouldn't end there. A massive fire tore through the structure in 1906 and completely gutted the building. Horses that pulled the equipment wagons were unable to climb the icy hill that led to the frat house.

Is this why Jennie lingers on, wandering the Cornell campus? Is this why her apparition has been seen in the tower?

Jennie has left more questions than answers for her beloved Cornell.

## Marroney Theatre—University of Arizona

### Gene the Ghost

More firsthand accounts about the University of Arizona's paranormal side stream in from the Marroney Theatre. As home to the university's first-class dramatic, comic, and musical productions, the theater has seen its share of characters, but none of those characters have engaged with students and faculty like Gene the Ghost.

Jeff Warburton, a theater professor, has no doubts. He believes the ghosts of Marroney aren't university legends or rumors; they're the real deal, or maybe the surreal deal.

"There are reportedly ghosts throughout the Marroney Theatre that I've had a few encounters with and that students have had encounters with as well," he told the student newspaper.

The spirit, tagged Gene the Ghost by students, has been spotted by students during performances. Usually, these theater ghosts are seen as either misty spirits or full-body apparitions of people who appear normal in most respects, but are dressed in clothes from a different time period.

But, Gene manifests in other ways, according to Warburton.

Once while the theater professor was alone, he heard footsteps. He's also felt a cool gust of wind rush past him, a telltale sign of a spirit's presence.

A far more bizarre incident offers an inkling to the spirit's mischievous personality. Warburton said he was in the auditorium when he realized he lost his keys. We all can relate to that feeling of panic that pulses through your body when your keys are missing. As Warburton searched frantically, he heard the sound in the seating area of the auditorium. It sounded like keys hitting the floor. Sure enough, when Warburton went to investigate, he found his keys lying on the floor.

The haunting at Marroney may be tied to Gene Lafferty, a former technical director at the theater. Hence, the name "Gene the Ghost."

But it could be that, as we've discovered with other haunted university theaters, creative folks can just tap into the supernatural more easily than other students.

Whether it's the ghost of a former director or just the psychic sensitivities of the University of Arizona's creative types, the spirit, or spirits are nothing to be scared of.

As Warburton puts it, "They're not harmful at all. You usually hurt yourself running like hell."

# Fisher Theater—Iowa State University

*There Are No Small Hauntings, Only Small Spirits*

Right in the middle of rehearsal, two students clearly heard someone shout out a name.

That's not unusual. Directors constantly shout out names and directions during run-throughs.

Except, the two drama students were the only ones on stage who clearly heard the name, "Dennis," shouted out from the empty theater.

There was another reason to be concerned that the shout had a human source: the incident occurred at Iowa State University's extremely haunted Fisher Theater.

Greg Henry, a theater director, said he was one of the students who heard the name being shouted. The other student was Dennis Ryan, who was starring in the production of *Amadeus*. But, according to Henry, that's not the only strange tale told about the theater.

Henry and others have more stories of weird encounters at Fisher Theater. The theater, a living laboratory for the university's theater students, is fairly young as haunted buildings go. Named after J. W. Fisher, a university benefactor, the 454-seat theater was completed in 1974.

Though it's new on the haunted-building scale, the paranormal phenomena witnessed in the theater are timeless examples of ghostly visits and interactions. Henry said that restless spirits move off the stage and into the seating area.

"I've heard the seats behind me move when I was sitting in the back of the theater," Henry said. "When I turn around, there's no one there."

In yet another encounter, a female student—the victim of a bad breakup with her boyfriend—was alone and having a good cry in the lighting booth. She left the booth. When she returned, she found a tissue waiting for her.

The tissue-from-beyond story has led some paranormal experts to conclude that the spirit haunting Fisher Theater is benevolent. Even welcoming.

As Henry puts it, the theater is "kind of a cold and sterile building. It's nice to know there's someone to keep it warm for us."

Henry and most witnesses don't need to speculate who is haunting the theater. The source of the haunting is Fredrica Shattuck, the force of nature (and now force of supernature) who spent 50 years in the early twentieth century driving the university to organize a theater program. Fredrica's efforts are legendary and they were acknowledged when the first theater at Iowa State was named the Shattuck Theater. Although the Shattuck Theater was torn down, students manage to keep her memory alive. The students still use her donated wheelchair as a prop—and it's been known to gently wheel down the stage, all on its own.

Sherry Hoopes, a theater professor in the late 1970s was there for one performance, according to a 1978 issue of the *Iowa State Daily*. According to the article, Hoopes and a bunch of cast members heard strange noises during rehearsals. They decided to investigate. What they saw shocked them. Fredrica's wheelchair had rolled by itself across the stage and turned to face the seats. It was like she was preparing to give a good soliloquy.

That's just like Fredrica, the students say—always stealing the scene.

## Purple Masque Theatre—Kansas State University
*Only at K-State Would a Football Player Haunt a Theater*
The Purple Masque Theatre is a weird little place.

First, the name is a little weird. What's up with the "Purple Masque?" The place is just asking to be haunted with a name like that.

Then, there's the location. It's situated in East Memorial Stadium, once the home of K-State's football team and reportedly the site of the first night college football game.

But what's really weird about the Purple Masque is that it's haunted. I know what you're thinking—there are dozens of haunted university theaters. Well, it's not so much that this theater is haunted; it's who is haunting it.

The Purple Masque Theatre is haunted by a dead football player that everyone's dubbed, Nick the Ghost. Nick's legend goes something like this: Nick was playing football for K-State when he was horribly injured during a game. The team's physicians rushed him off the field and transported him to the best place to work on the poor player—the stadium's cafeteria. That's where poor Nick finally succumbed.

It may sound like a typical campus legend, but several witnesses who have either worked in the theater or acted in one of the productions have stepped forward to say it's more than a legend.

Nick's presence is felt in several ways. Purses and books suddenly disappear and—just as suddenly—reappear, either back at the original spot, or somehow transported to another area of the theater. Lights in the theater have been known to blink on and off unexpectedly. Students also blame Nick for the inordinate amount of paint spills and other accidents.

One believer is a creative theater teacher at the Purple Masque. Sally Bailey said she believes that Nick the Ghost is behind some of the strange actions at the theater. But she wasn't always a believer.

She was once dismissive of Nick, but when the supernatural activity appeared to focus on her, she wised up.

Bailey tells this story:

"My first couple of years of teaching, there were a couple of times when I thought that my purse had disappeared, and then at the end of class or the end of rehearsal, it would show up back where I had originally put it. I decided that Nick was spiriting it away just to let me know he was around and that I'd better be respectful."

Since then, Bailey makes sure she offers a little Nick 101 to her students to appease the spirit.

"I think that he feels we are keeping his name alive and respecting his memory, so he doesn't feel the need to play tricks on me and my students."

It's a smart strategy because legend has it that Nick is very selective about whom he appears to. It seems that the less you believe in Nick, the more he will seek you out. Charlotte MacFarland, a K-State professor, wasn't a believer, either. Her experience in the 1970s changed her profoundly.

MacFarland said that one rainy evening during rehearsals of a production of *Nobody Like Us*, she saw the shape of a man at the stage door. The professor said he stepped in front of the light and she clearly saw a silhouette.

She got up and walked toward the stage. And the man disappeared.

MacFarland enlisted the help of the stage manager to try to find this interloper. They looked everywhere, scouring the building. They even looked under boxes. They double-checked the boxes—all of which were locked.

There was nobody there.

As MacFarland walked back to her car that night, the realization hit her. It wasn't a human who stepped in front of the lights that evening; it had to be a ghost.

As she tells it:

"I never bought into that kind of stuff; I just said it was theater people loving drama. But on the way back I thought, 'I think I'd rather it be a ghost than a person.' I don't like to think there was some creepy guy."

The next day, MacFarland confessed to a group of students that she had a run-in with Nick. But she still wasn't convinced. She dared Nick to appear, saying, "Nick, you really scared me last night. It doesn't matter because the truth is: I still don't believe in you."

The instant she said that a light over her head exploded.

Now the professor was convinced. And a little scared. She wouldn't go into the theater alone. If she arrived a little early for class, MacFarland waited for some other students to go in first. Then, she'd make her way into the theater.

Often, Nick isn't seen or heard—but felt.

Alice Warden, a K-State student, told a student newspaper reporter:

"There are times in which I have been alone in an area of the Masque and had the sudden feeling that someone was there with me," Warden said. "That's usually the feeling I get when a ghost is near me."

Professor MacFarland had the same experience:

"I just always felt like there was something there, I really did. A lot of it was just left over from my experience, but I really did feel like something was going on."

The theater professor said that eerie feeling faded over time. Maybe Nick has moved on to haunt other people. Perhaps Nick the Ghost and Charlotte MacFarland, like others who live in haunted houses or attend haunted universities, have learned how to live with each other.

There's been talk that the Purple Masque is moving, students worry about whether Nick will be displaced.

But a lot of students believe that Nick isn't going away, even if the theater does. Most students are convinced that Nick haunts the campus—not just a building.

"His connection isn't to the theater itself, it's the connection to that area on campus. I don't know if he will stick around and 'haunt' the new Welcome Center or not, whether he sticks around or not just depends on him, I guess."

## Washington Hall—University of Notre Dame
### *Win One for the Ghost of the Gipper*

> *"Some time, Rock, when the team is up against it, when things are wrong and the breaks are beating the boys, tell them to go in there with all they've got and win just one for the Gipper. I don't know where I'll be then, Rock. But I'll know about it, and I'll be happy."*—George Gipp

For Notre Dame students, alumni, and fans, Washington Hall and its imposing modern Gothic architecture is almost as iconic as touchdown Jesus—the statue of Christ with outstretched hands who looks down on Notre Dame's famed football stadium.

Located on what students call "the God Quad," the music and performing arts center is one of the oldest buildings on campus. Washington Hall also serves as a backdrop for most of the school's hallowed and haunted lore. For instance, it's on this spot that George "the Gipper" Gipp, the football legend, returned from a late-night outing and decided to sleep on the steps of Washington Hall, rather than venturing to his room and facing the wrath of the ever-watchful rector.

The freezing temperatures that night were blamed for the fever that swept through Gipp's body the following days. They certainly didn't help. Gipp eventually succumbed to the fever, his last words, urging his team to "win one for the Gipper," have inspired Notre Dame fans since.

It's not the only way the Gipper's presence is felt on campus, though, and his unfortunate death wasn't the only deadly incident at Washington Hall. In the late 1800s, a steeplejack fell off of Washington Hall and plummeted to his death.

Gipp and the unfortunate worker are just two spirit suspects who now reportedly haunt Washington Hall.

Probably the most famous encounter with Washington Hall's spectral suspects occurred shortly after Gipp's death in 1920. The story first appeared in a 1926 edition of the *Dome*, a Notre Dame student publication. According to the story, a Brazilian student lived in Science Hall. From his room in Science Hall, the student could see the entrance of Washington Hall. One night, the student looked out the window and saw a figure riding a white horse! He swore the figure was none other than George Gipp. Bryce Chung, a host for the Notre Dame ghost tour, doesn't think it was Gipp; he believes the figure on horseback was a Native American who was visiting the land of his ancestors. Chung said that Potawatomi Indians used to bury their dead on the two lakes on the Notre Dame campus.

The story of an equestrian spirit may seem a bit outlandish for Notre Dame. I mean, this isn't Oklahoma State. But the appearance seemed to jibe with other strange goings-on at the building.

Some students heard the long, loud monotone note of a horn blasting out in Washington Hall. It usually happened at midnight. The funny thing was the sound didn't seem to be coming from any specific room or hall; the sound was coming from within the building, itself.

Slamming doors and the sound of footsteps also joined the paranormal chorus at the music hall.

Washington Hall's paranormal hijinks became the talk of the campus. A few alumni have since stepped forward to claim that they were the ones behind the haunted horn blasts. But other students at the time counter those claims. Charles Davis told the *South Bend Tribune* in 1977 that he had ingeniously rigged the phantom horn. Davis said that he had access to the cupboard where the school stored musical instruments. By rigging up an enema hose to one of the horns in the cupboard, he could produce a near perfect B-flat note.

Mystery solved? Not so fast.

Clarence Manion, who went to school with Davis and was Dean of the Law School in the late 1970s, immediately saw flaws in Davis's testimony. He said that Davis lived in Scion, far away from Washington Hall. He couldn't be responsible for each incident. Manion also doubted another student who also claimed he caused the horn blast. Manion said he was with the student on at least one occasion when they heard the note blasting through Washington Hall.

Manion was steadfast. He wasn't sure what was behind the strange events at Washington Hall, but it wasn't simply a practical joke.

"I'm not ready to say that we all thought it was some sort of spiritual or other kind of exotic manifestation. We felt it must be a door, it must be something, something logical that could account for it and the consistency of its sound. But we could never explain the door slamming and the walking up the stairs, because I had lain in bed and listened. The door would slam, but the door was always locked. I didn't know what was causing it, but I never attributed it to the Devil or the spirit of George Gipp or that steeplejack or any of those things. But then when you heard the horn itself, there was no way to connect it with anything except that sustained, clear note...."

In the 1950s, a new wave of paranormal phenomena swept the music hall. This time, students swore they heard the sound of someone walking on the roof. When they went outside to investigate, they said there was no one on the roof and no sign that someone was doing work on the roof—no ladders or scaffolding, for example.

The clamor to solve the riddle of Washington Hall's spirits led to more and more student-run ghost hunts at the site. Not wanting a bunch of students—paranormal researchers, or not—stalking the halls late at night, the university promptly set a policy that Washington Hall would be closed at 11 p.m.

In 1986, some theatre students tested that policy in an attempt to make contact with whatever was haunting Washington Hall. After sneaking into the building, the group convened on the stage and pulled out a Ouija board.

When the students asked the ghost to identify itself, the board spelled out the initials, "S. G."

It was a bit befuddling. Suddenly, the indicator swung wildly across the board, spelling out "GOODBYE." To the group's amazement, the spirit repeated the message again: "GOODBYE."

Fearing the worst was about to happen, the collegiate ghost sleuths retreated to the nearest exit. They reconvened at a nearby parking lot. As they did, they noticed the door where they just exited opened. Standing at the open door was the security guard—or S. G. for short.

Notre Dame students and staff have a few more explanations for the strange happenings at Washington Hall. According to an article in *Notre Dame Magazine*, a priest who died while watching a movie in 1946 may be haunting the place.

These stories have filtered out from custodians and workers who have the night shift at the hall. Custodians say they have seen an elderly man that they describe as "Irish, balding, with reddish hair." It sounded like a perfect description of Brother Canute Lardner.

A custodian said that he noticed a man, perhaps a priest, looking out a first-floor window in Washington Hall one day. The priest turned to him and, in a thick Irish accent, asked, "Could you open the window please?"

The custodian demurred. "I don't think I know you."

"Oh, it's quite all right," the priest casually replied, "I'm with the building."

He's with the building in more ways than one—and so are the Gipper, Potawatomi warriors, and a few other stray spirits who keep Washington Hall one of the most haunted spots on the Notre Dame campus.

# ?

# SORORITIES AND FRATERNITIES

## When "Hell Week" Lasts a Little Longer than Expected...

Ever notice that the best horror movies take place at fraternity or sorority houses?

Maybe it's because we don't necessarily mind a few uppity rich kids get chased around by hatchet murderers.

But there may be another reason.

In campus ghost lore, paranormal terror is nothing new for frat brothers and sorority sisters. Ghosts, spirits, malevolent entities, and poltergeists all make appearances in stories about haunted Greek organizations.

Whether they're actually haunted or not is up for debate, but there's no question that frat houses look haunted. They're typically large homes with enough space to house a few dozen brothers or sisters and play host to social functions. The homes tend to have a lot of history—in some cases decades—attached to them and during that time there is a higher probability of some event happening that triggers paranormal activity.

Fraternities and sororities also create a seamless network to keep the stories active. As one group leaves the house, a new group comes in and is imbued with the tales of the supernatural. This is one reason that ghost lore spreads so easily in universities, but in the case of a fraternity or sorority, the effect is actually compounded because the group is small and inclusive.

But that raises another question: Could it be that fraternities and sororities are paranormally active because the best pranksters usually join Greek organizations and are good at keeping secrets?

Read on and judge for yourselves.

We start at the University of Maryland, a university with a couple of Greek ghosts attached.

## Kappa Delta, Alpha Omicron Pi, Delta Tau Delta— University of Maryland

### Brothers and Sisters in Spirit

The ghosts of the University of Maryland don't just hang out in the stoic old campus offices and classrooms—they like to socialize, too. There's no better place for the spirits of the dead to mingle with the living world than in one of the university's many fraternity and sorority houses.

The sisters of Kappa Delta told the student newspaper that their sorority house is haunted by a founder of the sorority, Alma Preinkert. A former university registrar and much-loved campus figure, the university community was devastated when she was found brutally murdered in her home in Washington, D.C. To make the incident even more tragic, the murder was never solved.

Several Kappa Delta sisters say they saw Alma in the sorority house, along with a long list of other "crazy paranormal things." In fact, the sisters said they saw a whole room full of ghosts of sorority girls past dancing on the sun deck! The house was closed at the time.

Not to be outdone, Alpha Omicron Pi members said their sorority is haunted. The list of the paranormal activity in their house is lengthy. Sisters and guests have heard eerie music play all by itself, computers operate on their own, and objects move and fall without anybody near them.

One member said she was shocked when she saw a pair of red eyes glaring at her.

Most sisters suspect a sorority sister who died in an automobile crash in the mid-'90s is haunting the house.

The ghost of a crash victim wouldn't be without precedent at the University of Maryland.

Back in 1955, a member of the Delta Tau Delta fraternity was killed in an car accident. Since then, the fraternity house has been the epicenter of weird events. And we're not just talking about the beginning-of-semester mixers.

Some of the phenomena included moving furniture and strange temperatures fluctuations. One cook, who had witnessed the moving furniture, was afraid to be in the kitchen.

Donald Jenkins, a student, told the Maryland state folklore project that while studying, he heard the sound of moving furniture. He immediately went to the scene of the commotion, expecting to see some prank-playing fraternity brothers. That's not what he found.

"I went running back there and I couldn't find anybody," he says. "So I heard some more chairs moving and I decided it was time to go to bed."

It wasn't the last time the ghost of the redecorating frat boy visited Jenkins. He said the next semester, the same thing happened all over again.

# Sigma Alpha Epsilon—University of Oregon

*Greek Ghosts and Poltergeists*

Lost items.

Teleported objects.

Phantom piano music.

These are either examples of paranormal activity, or evidence that a frat house has one of the best practical jokers of all times.

The members of Sigma Alpha Epsilon at the University of Oregon believe the latter and went to the student newspaper to plead that case. They even gave the spirit a name—Laurel. But there's another story that the ghost isn't the spirit of the pleasant-sounding Laurel. It may be a crime victim.

One manifestation occurred during winter break. Since most of the house residents had gone home for the holidays, the house—one of the largest houses in Eugene—stood quiet and empty. Just two brothers milled around the place.

According to one member, the brothers were on the house's second floor when they heard something. It sounded like someone was playing the piano on the first floor. But they knew that was impossible. Everyone had gone home for break. Maybe a brother missed his ride home? Maybe someone broke in to the frat house? But who breaks in and plays a few bars on the piano? It was a long shot, but the two—now creeped out—members decided to investigate.

By the time they walked downstairs and made it to the piano, the music had stopped. And the piano player apparently disappeared.

Was it Laurel?

Laurel, or whoever haunts the Sigma Alpha Epsilon house, has a devious side, too.

A brother said he placed his keys on a desk. He looked away for a second, and they were gone. He immediately tore the desk apart looking for the keys. As he reached the upper limits of his frustration, he heard the clinking of metal. The keys had somehow dropped out of thin air and landed in the middle of the room, far away from the desk where the set was last seen. This is typical poltergeist phenomena.

Some say that Laurel's appearance—and the poltergeist activity—is connected to a plaque. When the plaque is stolen, the activity ignites. Once the connection between Laurel and the plaque was made public, a few members of fellow fraternity and sorority organizations made it a point to snatch the plaque as a practical joke—and let their fellow Greeks at Sigma Alpha Epsilon pay the paranormal price.

Another tale indicates that the ghost has nothing to do with plaques or Laurel.

A member said that during a Ouija board session, a spirit revealed a totally different story about the origins of the paranormal activity in the frat house.

The spirit was a murder victim and was buried under the floorboards.

Did anyone bother to check the floorboards for a body?

It seems that bravery in the frat does have its limits.

## Sigma Phi Epsilon—Iowa State University
*No Monkeying Around with the Supernatural*

Universities play hosts to a lot of haunted fraternities and Iowa State is no different. The brothers at Sigma Phi Epsilon have dubbed a mysterious entity or poltergeist at their house, Monkey Boy.

Despite its funny-sounding moniker, Monkey Boy is reportedly behind some serious-sounding incidents. Members say that one time, while everyone was gathered in the main room to attend a fireside meeting, they heard the distinct sound of someone opening the third-floor door. But no one was on that floor. Then, moments later, the second-floor door mysteriously creaked open.

After they investigated, the brothers couldn't find anyone on the floors who might have caused the disturbance. They quickly blamed Monkey Boy, though. After all, he was blamed for other disturbances at the house, like slamming doors, throwing CDs, and cranking up stereos.

# Greek Ghosts—University of Ohio

## *Ohio Frats and Sororities Have Spirits—Yes They Do!*

Fraternities and sororities, even those connected to a national chapter, have a tendency to take on the culture of their own university. So it comes as absolutely no surprise that frats and sororities at Ohio University are deeply embedded with paranormal stories.

Residual energies and interactive spirits are common in the buildings and houses that make up Ohio University's Greek community.

We'll start with a ghost who supposedly haunts the Sigma Phi Epsilon House.

### Sigma Phi Epsilon

Sigma Phi wasn't the first frat to be headquartered in the building. In fact, a few fraternities and sororities called this site home. In a few minutes, you'll probably figure out why the former brothers and sisters were so quick to pass the building on to another unsuspecting Greek organization.

It's Nicodemus's fault.

Nicodemus is supposedly a ghost of a former slave who escaped into Ohio through the informal collection of safe houses now referred to as the Underground Railroad. The extensive use of safe houses in Athens is another reason paranormal experts suggest that the city and the university are so haunted. Escaping to the north was a painful, fearful journey—all emotions that can tie spirits to a building or piece of ground.

Nicodemus may have escaped slavery, but the tales from Sigma Phi indicate his spirit is still trapped in the earthly plane.

But Nicodemus isn't merely a residual energy. He appears to be an interactive spirit with a mischievous side.

One firsthand encounter with Nicodemus involved Josh Kalaman, a sophomore history student who was living at the house. Kalaman said that he had heard about the haunting and knew about Nicodemus. Then he experienced something that he—or his brothers—could never explain.

Kalaman said he was sleeping early one morning when his bed sheets were pulled off. He thought it might be a prank, but he was sleeping in the top bunk, so it would be no easy prank to pull off. Kalaman checked, and there was no one else in the room.

The sheets were pulled off a few times that morning.

He never found an explanation for the sheet-shorting activity, at least not a natural one. Kalaman said other phenomena are just as inexplicable.

"Every now and then lights will flicker, and sometimes an Xbox will turn on and sign in to a profile. People talk about stuff being moved on their shelves and doors slamming, too."

Prior to Sigma Phi moving in, the Zeta Tau Alpha sorority lived with Nicodemus. His antics, especially back in the 1970s, became the stuff of Ohio University legend and were documented in an *Athens Magazine* article. The sisters reported wild activity. Weird noises were heard. Doors and cabinets would suddenly fly open. Sisters said they could feel something—or someone—touching them.

Then, there was the scratching.

Residents said they could hear scratching behind the walls in one section of the building that supposedly holds a passageway used by slaves as they stayed at the safe house. The activity appeared to verify one aspect of the Nicodemus legend. The legend said that Nicodemus was hiding in the secret passageway when slave bounty hunters found him and, later, shot him.

Despite the presence of a dead, non-dues-paying frat member, the Sigma Phi brothers said they weren't afraid of Nicodemus.

Kalaman told the *Ohio University Post*, "I don't feel threatened at all. Sometimes if you go downstairs late at night you get kind of an uneasy feeling, but no one feels threatened. And we always joke that, 'Oh, he gets to live in a frat house. He's probably loving it.'"

### PHI BETA PHI

If there's one thing that can be said about the spirits that haunt the considerably haunted Ohio University, it's that they're equal-opportunity spooks. They have no compunction against scaring males or females.

The Pi Beta Phi house is supposedly haunted.

Catie Carroll, a student who lived in the house, told a reporter that a sister detailed what paranormal experts would call an "audible" spirit. Carroll said that the sorority member was laying in bed one night when she heard a strange noise. It sounded like someone was singing the ABCs. But it couldn't be another sister. This voice sounded exactly like a little girl.

She decided to investigate and went to the spot where the sound was originating. That's when she saw a shadow and retreated back to the bed. The singing only stopped when the sister pulled the cover over her head and began to scream

The scream didn't scare the ghosts away for long, though. Carroll reported more supernatural run-ins at the sorority house.

"We've been sleeping, and we've felt someone crawl into bed with us and get under the covers. I turned over when it happened and there was no one there—it sounds so weird—but it happened to me one time and I told my roommate and she said it has happened to her, too."

So, who's haunting the Pi Beta Phi house?

The most likely culprit is a young girl who drowned in a swimming pool.

But, like a surprise raid on a college keg party, the list of suspects continues to grow.

### DELTA TAU DELTA

We all know that houses can be haunted. Dorms and classrooms can be haunted. Administrative buildings and university museums can be haunted. But, can simple objects be haunted?

If you ask the brothers at Delta Tau Delta house at Ohio University, they're likely to agree with paranormal experts who suggest that objects can be just as haunted as your typical, old neighborhood Victorian mansion that was the site of a murder-suicide.

Objects—from rocks to dolls, from sticks to religious works—can be infused with supernatural powers.

In the case of Ohio's Delta Tau Delta, a scavenger trip to a local haunted cemetery in Athens ended up unleashing a storm of paranormal activity.

According to one story, a group of brothers traveled to the Simms Cemetery, supposedly one of the town's most haunted spots. They, unwisely, took a chunk of tombstone home with them as a memento of the adventure.

It turned out that they brought home a little piece of whatever spirits haunt the Simms Cemetery.

Soon after, strange events began to occur. Those brothers in the know quickly diagnosed the problems as poltergeist activity. Objects went missing. Strange noises erupted at night. There were even tales of objects moving without any source pushing or pulling the item.

Using a little deductive reasoning, the fraternity members traced the problems back to their little cemetery souvenir. They packed the stone and placed it back in its original spot in the graveyard.

Apparently, the ghost was appeased. By all reports, the paranormal activity abated since then.

# 8

## HAUNTED PEOPLE
## AND THINGS

We know that buildings can be haunted, and we've just discovered that the ground itself can be spiritually active. Graveyards and battlefields are some of the most active spots on campus.

But, are there such things as haunted people and haunted things?

Actually, ghost lore—and especially campus ghost lore—indicates that there are haunted people. Famous people or campus celebrities are among the most likely stars of these ghostly tales. For instance, naval hero John Paul Jones has been seen around the campus of the Naval Academy—a few hundred years after his death.

But there are other characters who can become paranormal free-lancers, able to drift from building to building and from place to place.

Sometimes the ghost manages to work his or her way off campus and take up residence in a nearby building. In the pages ahead, we'll investigate a theater that supposedly is haunted by a former university student.

There is a whole paranormal study area that focuses on haunted and cursed objects. If you've ever heard of a ghost of a loved one appearing once an object from that person is brought into a home, you probably have a good idea of what a haunted object is. But there are others: dolls that seem to move by themselves or the souvenir that seems to precipitate a string of bad luck.

In the ghost lore of colleges and universities, there are stories about haunted objects. Chimes that can attract paranormal activity and statues that offer supernatural powers lead the list of haunted campus objects.

Our first story is about a student who seemed a little aimless in life. It's no wonder he drifted off campus a little.

## Guthrie Theater—
## Ghost of a University of Minnesota Student
*Work-Life… Or Work-Afterlife?*

With tuition, food, room and board, not to mention the ever-present need for beer money, most University of Minnesota students deliver pizzas, stack books at the library, sell clothes, or do whatever they have to do to keep up with these expenses.

You probably won't find too many students who will tell you they like these side gigs. But, if you believe stories about the Guthrie Theater, a supposedly haunted theater located in Minneapolis, at least one University of Minnesota student loved his part-time job so much that even death couldn't keep him from it.

According to one version of the story, a university student, sometimes identified as Richard Miller, worked as an usher in the late 1960s. About two days after the student quit the job, he tragically committed suicide. When the body was discovered, the student was neatly attired in his usher uniform and, even more peculiar, in a note found nearby, he asked to be buried in his usher uniform.

Since then, the theater has never been the same.

The stories of encounters with a ghostly usher began to trickle in almost immediately after the tragic death. According to Robert T. Smith, a columnist for the *Minneapolis Tribune*, one woman came up to a Guthrie Theater usher to complain about the other usher, who insisted on walking up and down the aisles during the play.

It was quite disturbing, she said.

She had no idea.

The usher was a bit taken aback by the customer's complaint. He had been the only usher in the area and hadn't seen any other staff members in the aisle. So he asked her to describe this inconsiderate usher. She described Richard Miller exactly—she even mentioned the mole on his face.

Smith interviewed a member of the theater's management, who told him, "There was no one in our employ at the time that fit the description, but it fit the dead young man perfectly."

Guthrie's haunted usher apparently isn't satisfied with policing the aisles. He longs to be on stage. Two men said that when they were asked (or forced, more likely) to stay overnight at the theater to repair the air conditioning unit, they were startled to hear the sound of someone tapping out notes on the piano. When they looked up, they saw a misty form undulate through the door and hover above them. One of the horrified workers said he saw the form take the shape of a face, a face that stared at them.

Sometimes, jobs aren't really worth the money. You can forgive these two workers for deciding the unemployment line was better than the overnight shift at the Guthrie.

While reports of a ghostly usher are reported in various sections of the theater, aisle 18 seems to be the hub of paranormal activity. Besides seeing a filmy shape wearing clothes from another era pacing back and forth during performances, people have also seen objects move without visible means of support.

A group of ushers decided to take matters in their own hands. Hoping to find out who was behind the strange ghost lights in the halls and other weird phenomena, the employees pulled out a trusty Ouija board one night after they closed and asked who was haunting the theater.

The response: DIK MILLER.

The spelling, the employees agreed, was pretty close to the name of one of the spirit suspects, Richard Miller.

Actors aren't immune to the haunting, either. During rehearsals, more than one actor has glanced into the mostly empty theater and caught sight of a college-aged boy in odd clothes taking in the show.

How, they wonder, did this kid get in the locked theater?

Simple. He never left.

## Ezra Cornell's Family—Cornell University
### *The Haunted Roots of Cornell's Founder*

The roots of the Cornell family are well-established, burrowing deeply into the very founding of America. Stories of the Cornell family ghosts start around that time, too.

The Cornells were a pioneering family among pioneers who settled the nation.

That's why the news spread fast in 1672—despite the primitive news distribution of the time—that Rebecca Cornell had been found dead in their home in Connecticut. She had been burned to death.

Since her body was found by the fireplace, the initial speculation was that an ember from the fireplace had landed on Rebecca's clothes and ignited. It was a common enough death in the seventeenth century. The matter was quickly settled. The death was an accident.

Until the ghost of Rebecca appeared.

Rebecca's brother, John Briggs, told the local magistrate that he woke up in the night to see his departed sister in front of him. With the "light of heaven around her," Rebecca simply said, "I am your sister Cornell," and twice said, "see how I was burnt with fire." For Briggs, the visitation meant only one thing: Rebecca's death was no accident.

The magistrate agreed and sent the CSI unit of the time to examine Rebecca's body again. They discovered a small stab wound. Suspicion soon fell on Rebecca's son, Thomas Cornell. What is especially interesting about this paranormal intervention is that John Briggs actually testified of his sister's ghostly visit during the trial. The apparition may have sealed his nephew's fate.

Thomas was condemned and hanged.

Paranormal researchers like to debate the reasons behind ghostly apparitions. One theory is that ghosts, especially interactive spirits like Rebecca Cornell, are on a mission. They seek to address a wrong or seek justice. That theory certainly appears to apply to Rebecca's supernatural testimony. Once the accused killer met his end, there have been no more reports of Rebecca's ghost. Her home is haunt-free.

The same cannot be said about Cornell University. Plenty of ghosts stalk the university founded by Rebecca's descendant.

In our next story, though, we'll discover that not only do ghosts stalk Cornell, some folks from Cornell stalk ghosts!

Cornell's other haunted persona isn't really a ghost, so much as a ghost whisperer. Read on for a tale about the nutty professor and his haunted chats.

## Hiram Corson—Cornell University

*Cornell Faculty Member Channels a Society of Dead Poets*

Let's be honest. Professors can be nutty.

And Ivy League professors can be Ivy League nutty.

As an example, we needn't look any farther than Cornell's famous professor of Anglo-Saxon and English literature—Hiram Corson. Corson taught those subjects in the nineteenth century.

While some professors have the ability to make the words of Shakespeare and other great English writers come alive, Corson said he went one step farther; he made the actual writers come alive.

Corson said he was able to commune with a number of dead writers. He claimed to have talked with Alfred Tennyson, Walt Whitman, Henry Wadsworth Longfellow, and Robert Browning. He called them his "spirit visitors."

Corson's talks on literature always drew a crowd. When he discussed one of his favorite writers, his audience members remarked that it was almost like the professor was remembering a past encounter with a friend, not a long-dead literary figure.

Sometimes that rapport is unmistakeable. Once, after leading a discussion with a group about his visits with Browning, the room echoed with several loud raps. The audience was stunned, but the paranormal professor knew it was just the spirit of Browning signaling his pleasure with Corson's exploration of the poet's work.

Fortunately for students, Corson never asked the members of his dead-poet society to help him grade papers.

From a dead-poet society, we'll now reveal a dead-soldier society at West Point and prove that dead soldiers really don't die, they become haunted statues.

## General John Sedgwick—West Point

*Magic Spurs Are Supernatural Cheat Sheets for West Point Cadets*

Gen. John Sedgwick was not one for supernatural chitchat.

Maybe he should have been more open-minded.

One of the Union's great generals, Sedgwick knew that their commanding the high ground over the battle of Gettysburg gave them the strategic advantage over his Confederate foes. They must be held at all cost. But his men were scared. The threat of Confederate sharpshooters forced them to hunker down behind stones and trees.

Sedgwick was having none of it.

Pish-poshing the threat of some supernatural shot, he strode to the center of a clearing and told his men, "They couldn't hit an elephant at this distance."

The men heard a sharp report and as Sedgwick pronounced the word, "elephant," he fell dead. A sharpshooter had felled the great general.

Now, a monument to the Union general with an ironic sense of timing and wording stands on the campus of the United States Military Academy. The cool thing about the statue is that the spurs can spin freely.

There's a legend on campus that the spurs have a supernatural power. If a cadet is afraid of failing a class, they're instructed to dress in full parade uniform at midnight before the test and spin the statue's spurs.

If they do this right, the academically challenged cadets will feel that "even an elephant could pass that test," to paraphrase General Sedgwick.

## Lieutenant Sutton's Spirit—U.S. Naval Academy
*The Mystery of the Murdered Officer*

It was on October 13, 1907, that Lt. James Sutton and some of his friends decided to have a nightcap at a local saloon. I'm pretty sure you know that sailors don't just have a nightcap. One beer led to another and one whiskey led to a couple and pretty soon, bad things began to happen.

According to some versions of the tale, Sutton, who was actually a Marine stationed at the academy, and another sailor began to brawl. Sutton's temper boiled. His friends could barely restrain him. They hoped he'd cool off once they'd get the enraged officer back to the academy. But, in a sudden rage, he grabbed pistols and began to fire wildly.

Then, some witnesses claimed that they saw Sutton take a pistol, place the end of the barrel on his temple, and pull the trigger.

The Lieutenant fell dead.

But, this wasn't the end of the story—nor, presumably, was it the end of the Lieutenant.

Officially, the death was suicide due to a mental breakdown. But, Sutton's friends and family were not happy with this conclusion. There was just something wrong with it. Sutton, by all accounts, was a happy, well-adjusted guy, they said. Why would he shoot himself?

And then they began to hear rumors.

Whispers were passed around the Academy that Sutton had not killed himself at all. He was bludgeoned to death by the butt of one of the pistols.

Hushed whispers were one thing, but then news broke that Sutton's mother, who lived hundreds of miles away from the Naval Academy, received a visit from the lead witness—Sutton, himself. His mother said that Sutton's apparition appeared to her during the night of the incident. He told her that he was beaten and then another officer shot him.

Mom Sutton and her family demanded a real autopsy.

The results startled the Academy and those nonbelievers who scoffed at the idea that a spirit could wander hundreds of miles from the spot of its death and convey a message to family members.

The autopsy revealed that Lieutenant Sutton was, in fact, beaten.

Despite this victory, ultimate justice was never meted out. The shooter was never identified.

Some say that because the killer was never found, the ultimate mission of Lieutenant Sutton continues to this day. His restless spirit has been spotted by midshipmen. Sutton's spirit doesn't seem tied to one place either—he wanders throughout the campus. Midshipmen have claimed that they've been awoken in the deep hours of night or the wee hours of the morning by some dark, foreboding feeling. When they open their eyes and adjust to the light, they say they've seen the dead officer staring at them, face to face. He's usually described by credible witnesses as "hovering" over them.

A few recent accounts have him walking along a fence that borders the Naval Academy. Some say they've seen a strange light that appears to go right through the wall.

Not all are convinced that this is the ghost of Lieutenant Sutton. It could be another campus spirit.

But, midshipmen do admit, crashing through a wall instead of using a perfectly good door does indeed seem to be something that a Marine would do.

Another ghost is crashing the party at the Naval Academy and this one can pull rank on just about anyone in the services.

## The Ghost of John Paul Jones—U.S. Naval Academy
*I Have Not Yet Begun To Haunt!*

If there's any single military figure that best exemplified the fighting spirit of the men and women of the U.S. Naval Academy, it's John Paul Jones.

The famous Revolutionary War naval hero never surrendered, whether it was surrendering his ship to the English, or, apparently, his soul to the great beyond.

John Paul Jones was born in 1747, but it wasn't until the American Revolution that Jones became famous as a naval warrior. The American Navy, when Jones signed on to help, was just a few ships and they were matched up against the full might of the world's best and biggest naval power—the British Navy.

Vastly outnumbered and woefully unprepared, what did Jones do? He went on the offensive, of course, leading a raiding mission on England, itself, while commanding the sloop-of-war, the Ranger. Jones's successful raid on England made him famous, or infamous, depending on what side of the pond you were from.

While captain of the Bonhomme Richard, Jones got in a tussle with an English ship. The captain of the ship demanded Jones surrender.

He replied with his famous, "I have not yet begun to fight." And he was right. Jones prevailed and another chapter was closed in the famous warrior's lengthy legend.

There are those people—especially the midshipmen at the Naval Academy—who say that the final chapter of the John Paul Jones legend has never fully been closed. In 1913, Jones was re-interred in a sarcophagus within the Naval Academy Chapel.

His spirit immediately went on the offensive.

One story is that Jones tested the daily honor guard who watches over Jones's crypt.

The guard told superiors that while on duty, he heard a voice ask his name. Initially, he refused to turn around. How could anyone be behind him? He didn't see anyone walk in and there were no entrances behind him.

Finally, curiosity began to chip away at the rigid spirit of the honor guard. He turned around and saw the spirit of a man dressed in an old naval uniform. The guard knew enough about Jones to immediately recognize the similarities between the presence that stood before him and the historic paintings and drawings of Jones.

The ghost repeated his question.

"What is your name?"

The guard stammered his name.

Once his request was granted, the phantom war hero nodded and walked out of the chapel, fading away as he reached the door.

Sightings of John Paul Jones continue. He's usually seen in the chapel or wandering the grounds.

What's he looking for?

Knowing Jones, he's looking for a way to find his war-sloop, Ranger, so he can re-join his beloved U.S. Navy.

We now move to haunted objects; our first is a bunch of elevators that, some say, will take you from the first floor and drop you off into the supernatural.

# The Fighting Illini's Haunted Elevators— University of Illinois

*Haunted Campus Elevators Going Up…*
*Spirits, Ghosts, Poltergeists…*

Communication 362 is a popular class on folklore. Specifically, it's a class on how folklore is used as communication. With a campus full of ghosts, spirits, and poltergeists, the University of Illinois is ideally suited for the class.

Comm 362 students gather and discuss campus folklore. The ghost stories of the University of Illinois range from the frightening to the funny, from the realistic to the outlandish.

The class isn't all popcorn and tall tales. Class members aren't just expected to retell stories they have heard from fellow students, alumni, and faculty; they also try to figure out why these stories were created and spread among the student body in the first place. Are they real encounters, or are they just works of fiction? If they are just fictional tales, why do they have such appeal?

One of the stories that no doubt inspires major debate among the students in the folklore class during the semester is the spirits that seem to attach to elevators at various buildings on campus, particularly the Natural Resources Building and the A. A. Harding Band Building.

## NATURAL RESOURCES BUILDING

Our first stop on the tour of haunted Illini elevators is at the Natural Resources Building. The tales reportedly started with a graduate student who told friends that while working late at the building, he heard the rumble of the elevator, apparently descending to a lower floor. Since he was all alone, he was curious. Maybe someone was coming to visit. He rose from his desk, walked to the hall, and waited for the elevator.

It finally reached his floor. The door remained closed for a few suspenseful seconds that seemed like an ominously long wait. When the doors opened, the student looked into an empty elevator.

If the time it took to open the doors seemed ominous, staring at an empty elevator ticked by in agonizingly creepy eternity. The elevator seemed to beckon him for a ride. He didn't accept. Finally, as if miffed at the rejection, the elevator doors slammed shut. The student listened as the elevator rose back to its original position.

Maybe it was just a mechanical glitch. Or somebody pulling a prank on him. Probably a mean senior.

After a while, the incident was filed away into the dim reaches of the student's memory. But one more encounter with the ghostly elevator cemented the building's paranormal activity in this man's memory forever.

Like the first incident, a graduate student once again found himself in the Natural Resources Building alone at night. Done with his work, he climbed into the elevator and pressed the floor number. Rumors of that initial encounter shuddered into his thoughts as soon as the elevator door shut. The door seemed to close aggressively—like it was mad.

He pressed the button to take him to a certain floor. Only the light of that floor was lit.

But, instead of going to the requested floor, the elevator stopped at every floor. The doors slowly opened, revealing empty halls. Then it would snap shut to continue its terrifying journey.

When the elevator finally reached his floor, the student didn't wait. He quickly exited, vowing that he would never ride the building's haunted elevator again. The stairs would be better for both his physical and mental health.

The student asked around the next couple of days. He talked to fellow students, graduate students, and even faculty members. Afraid that people would think he was a nut, the student was careful to shroud his inquiries in an innocent question: "Ever have trouble with the elevators in this place?"

The answers astonished him: most people he queried definitely experienced some "problems" with the elevator including riderless elevators, unexpected floor visits, and, in one case, the elevator entirely skipped the requested floor, but stopped on all the others.

A research assistant told a paranormal investigator of a similar incident. The researcher was finishing up his duties as a curator in the Ichthyology Department on the building's ground floor. He was often the last person in the building and—because of his class schedule—was forced to work late nights. On more than one occasion, he heard the elevator engage, drift down to another floor, and open its doors. But nobody was onboard.

Initially, the skeptical researcher dismissed the bizarre elevator behavior as nothing more than a mechanical glitch. But this was a guy who knew a thing or two about research. He noticed that the elevator never made unexpected stops when he was in the building during the morning or afternoon—only during the night and usually when he was alone. Mechanical glitches, the researcher noted, do not know the difference between night and day.

There were some factors that tied the incidents together: they all happened at night and they all happened when the witnesses were alone. Was it just a coincidence, an elevator on the fritz, or could it be some elevators can not only transport riders from floor to floor, but also from dimension to dimension?

## A. A. HARDING BAND BUILDING

Music is one way we connect with spirits, and sometimes that bond can turn downright physical. The Harding Band Building is headquarters for the University of Illinois' amazing band program. It also houses some interesting archives of famous marching band composer John Philip Sousa.

The archive is stored on the upper level of the band building. That's bad news for students and faculty members trying to avoid Harding Band Building's spooky elevator. Students and faculty members say there's something peculiar about the elevator, specifically the smell.

People say they smell pipe smoke—even though there's not a pipe smoker in sight and, with the strict rules against tobacco in campus buildings, it's doubtful that a pipe smoker has been in the building for years.

Jeff McManus, a University of Illinois student, said that students blame a ghost for the supernatural smell.

"There's this one guy who used to smoke a pipe in the elevator. Some students say they smell pipe smoke in the elevator."

The pipe-smoking ghost makes his presence known in other ways, including some poltergeist-type activities. Doors continually slam, even after closing hours, when students have technically cleared out. Some late-night visitors have even claimed to see the doors closing.

McManus added, "One of the band directors heard the doors closing. A lot were open and they all started closing in a row. There was no one else there."

So are all these elevators really haunted?

Folklore students find a variety of theories for the uberhaunted University of Illinois campus. Susan Davis, who teaches a class in folklore and campus storytelling, said that stories, like the haunted elevator, are ways for students to "attach themselves" to a campus.

"I think that legends, especially about physical places, are our ways of attaching ourselves to the campus," Davis said, "making it feel like a place that we belong to, that we fit into, and that we know something intense or personal about—that it's not such a huge, anonymous place, which it can seem, especially to freshmen."

Whether a dead student could attach himself or herself to an elevator, well, that's a subject for another class.

# Washington Avenue Bridge—
# University of Minnesota

*Bridge Over Haunted Waters*

The bridge between folklore and the actual supernatural can be a thin, shaky span to be sure, especially when it comes to tales of haunted campuses. One University of Minnesota student writes that he found that out the hard way one early morning while walking to work.

As fate would have it, the trek to work would take the student right over the Washington Avenue Bridge, a bridge that not only connects the University of Minnesota's East and West campuses, but is also one of the Twin Cities most haunted spots.

It was still dark, around 5:40 a.m., when the student started to cross the bridge over the Mighty Mississippi.

A man appeared on the opposite side of the bridge and was walking toward him. The two figures were the sole pedestrians on the great bridge.

As the man neared, the student felt an icy chill. Maybe it was just a cold wind drifting off the river.

Then the man suddenly and inexplicably disappeared in front of the wide eyes of the student.

Most people are in no rush to get to work, but when you witness the supernatural, a long day of drudgery seems a little more palatable. The student "bolted" off the bridge.

We could attribute this story to the high spirits of youth, or just a made-up tale aimed at keeping a cherished student legend alive for one more class.

But these stories are so common among area residents and university students that even paranormal experts wonder if there isn't something to the legend of the Washington Avenue Bridge.

The legend goes something like this:

Throughout the centuries, Old Man River, who has solemnly flowed under the Univerity of Minnesota's infamous bridge, has been more than a source of transportation for the nation's heartland; it's also the source of a steady stream of legends and ghost stories. The river's gift for folklore is just as generous with university students.

When you see the Washington Avenue Bridge for the first time, you realize it's unique. Weird, even. It has two decks—one for pedestrians and one for vehicles. The two-deck design makes it much taller than normal bridges. It also makes it more deadly.

That precarious height has built up the bridge's reputation that it not only connects the campuses, it serves as a connection between life and the afterlife. Deaths—both accidental and intentional—have been reported at the bridge.

The bridge's most famous suicide victim is, arguably, John Allyn Berryman, a Pulitzer Prize-winning poet and one of the university's prestigious professors. Berryman, who suffered from depression and alcoholism, jumped off the bridge in 1972.

Berryman's death was not swift or tidy; according to newspaper reports, he missed the water and landed in the flats where he died not by drowning, or trauma, but from suffocation.

According to the *Minnesota Daily*, the university's newspaper, his tragic death is just one of seven strange deaths that have occurred on or near the Washington Avenue Bridge. A recently released psychiatric patient died here, as did a student who was spray-painting the name of a girl before accidentally falling, the paper claims.

Students say this legacy of deaths is the cause of paranormal activity on the bridge. Witnesses say that they hear weird noises or the echo of footsteps while walking on the bridge alone. There are reports of cold spots and mysterious breezes. In another incident, flags were ripped off of the bridge, even though the bridge had been under surveillance.

Then there are those stories that just won't go away. Stories of a ghost that appears suddenly out of the mist and walks alone on the bridge, only to vanish an instant later.

Sound familiar?

Just some edgy student nerves? A couple university pranksters having fun and maybe stealing a couple flags?

Maybe, but there are a lot of people who would just as soon skip through a graveyard or stay the night in a haunted hotel before they cross the Washington Avenue Bridge by themselves.

## Bascom Hill—University of Wisconsin
### *Where the Dead Don't Rest in Peace*

The University of Wisconsin has a triple threat in haunted spots in Bascom Hill: a sacred hill, a haunted statue, and the graves of two campus workers who died accidentally on the job.

Geologists will tell you that Bascom Hill, besides being the centerpiece of the University of Wisconsin's campus, is a drumlin, a unique formation molded by glacial deposits nearly 20,000 years ago.

But if you ask students or other believers in the paranormal who've walked the hill at night, or were caught after hours in one of the notoriously haunted buildings, they'll tell you that Bascom Hill isn't just a drumlin; it's haunted. And if you don't believe them, ask the two guys who are in the graves, marked with simple plaques, underneath the statue of Abraham Lincoln at the top of Bascom Hill.

The two graves hold (sometimes) Samuel Warren, who was killed by lightning in 1838, and W. Nelson, who died in 1837. They both were among the first white settlers in Madison and were working on the capitol when they succumbed, according to campus lore. They haven't entirely settled, though. There are those who say these two permanent residents of Bascom Hill are responsible for the strange happenings. Witnesses have seen filmy images walking across the hill.

Other people have had more terrifying encounters.

Ying Chan, one proud University of Wisconsin alumna, was taking her relative from Taiwan on a tour of Bascom Hill. When the two approached Lincoln's statue, Chan's relative suddenly asked to leave the area—immediately.

Somewhat taken aback by the request, Chan pressed her relative why she wanted to leave. Was it something she said? Something she did?

But the woman eventually told Chan that as she looked up at the statue of Lincoln, she saw two figures smiling back at her.

The interesting part of this story is that Chan told the alumni magazine that she never knew that the graves—the graves of two men, to be exact—existed on Bascom Hill. She only learned about the existence of the graves after reading a story in the student newspaper much later. If a University of Wisconsin grad didn't realize that there were graves at the site, there is little chance that a relative from Taiwan had possessed this knowledge.

There's another layer to the theory that Bascom Hill is haunted. Bascom Hall, situated on its namesake's hill, is also apparently haunted. Reports and rumors have filtered through the university that, late at night, you can hear whispers, which some attribute to Mr. Warren and Mr. Nelson, while others say it's the chatting of construction workers who have left the premises a long time ago. Then again, other people— people who are definitely no fun—say that the whispers are nothing more than the building's really good acoustics.

Luckily, Bascom Hill has many suspects besides the spirits of Mr. Warren and Mr. Nelson and a ghostly scrum of chatty construction workers. Experts in paranormal investigation have wondered whether the presence of Native American burial sites haven't turned the dial up on supernatural activities. There's another more presidential suspect—Abraham Lincoln. The stoic site of Lincoln's statue at the top of Bascom Hill has spurred several rumors that the Great Emancipator himself is visiting the grounds of the University of Wisconsin.

Maybe he could swap the top hat for the cheesehead hat?

A new hat might be nice at Cornell University, too. It might help cover up all those brains in the university's famous, creepy collection of gray matter.

# Uris Hall—Cornell University

*Killer Brain Collection*

Each college has a collection of brains. You know the type: high SAT overachievers that pack their schedules with 20-plus credits, make the Dean's List each semester, and join every academic frat possible.

I know. I hate them, too.

Cornell has a brain collection of a totally different sort; it's a collection of brains—real, gray matter brains.

The brain collection is stored in Uris Hall, home to the university's Psychology Department.

One of the brains has a killer reputation. Edward Rulloff was a mild-mannered schoolteacher with a bit of a rage issue. One day, Rulloff asked his neighbor to help him move a large trunk into his carriage. The neighbor grew suspicious. Rulloff, after all, claimed his wife and infant had vanished.

Authorities arrested Rulloff. They believed that Rulloff killed his wife and child during a blind rage. He may have dumped the body into Cayuga Lake, but no one ever found the bodies. Without the bodies, the police couldn't charge Rulloff with murder, so they opted to charge him with kidnapping.

Rulloff escaped from jail and went on an apparent homicidal spree. He was eventually arrested for killing a man in Binghamton and convicted during a trial that was the O. J. Simpson courtroom drama of its era.

Rulloff was the last person publicly hanged in New York.

Just before Rulloff's date with the hangman in May 1871, he offered a jailhouse interview. During the interview, far from showing remorse, he offered this creepy promise:

"You cannot kill an unquiet spirit, and I know that my impending death will not mean the end of Rulloff. In the dead of night, walking along Cayuga Street, you will sense my presence. When you wake to a sudden chill, I will be in the room. And when you find yourself alone at the lake shore, gazing at gray Cayuga, know that I was cut short and your ancestors killed me."

Indeed Rulloff's ghost has been seen wandering the banks of the Cayuga.

Rulloff has also been pinned for another dark Cornell tradition. Over the years, the magnificent gorge that provides the students with such impressive views has also been the scene of terrible misfortunes. Several students have committed suicide by leaping off the gorge. In most cases, the deaths were unexpected. Because those who harbor suicidal thoughts often hide their depression, families and friends of the victims say they never showed any signs of self-destructive behavior.

You may never hear this publicly, but students have whispered among themselves another reason for the student deaths: it's Edward Rulloff's revenge.

## The Cincinnati Observatory Center— University of Cincinnati

*Watching the Skies, Talking to Heaven?*

When a University of Cincinnati environmental-health professor decided to make a call to the Cincinnati Observatory Center, she expected that she might get the answering machine message. She had no idea that on that day her call would be re-routed to the other side.

Who knows what ran through the professor's mind before she dialed the number? Maybe she had heard the rumors that the observatory, run by the University of Cincinnati and one of the first professionally operated observatories in the country, was haunted. The tale is well-known. According to local legend, a professor committed suicide in the observatory by hanging himself from one of the telescopes back in the 1940s.

After a few rings, the professor expected the answering machine to switch on. It didn't. Instead, the professor listened in horror as a strange, garbled voice answered her call. But she couldn't make out what the voice was saying.

There was an easy explanation: the answering machine was broken. But when she called back, she discovered to her dismay that the answering machine had never been turned on. Intrigued she deepened her investigation. Her investigation uncovered one weird fact: the day that she called was the anniversary of the poor astronomer's suicide.

But that's only one story.

Since then, people have reported seeing and hearing a ghost at the observatory on Mount Lookout that's often called the birthplace of American astronomy.

One of the groups that paid a visit to the observatory was the Spiritual H.O.P.E. society, a Cincinnati-based paranormal research team. During two investigations, one in 2009 and one in 2010, the group gathered some convincing evidence that some type of spirit—or maybe spirits—had made the observatory a resting spot on their own interrupted journey to the heavens.

Some of the team used electronic voice phenomena (EVP) techniques to record voices, some of whom sounded like children. The team distinctly heard one voice say, "Mommy," on the recording. Another voice said something like, "Door to hell."

More members claimed to hear strange music in the halls—phenomena not typically associated with this type of haunting.

For some other investigators, the spirits got up close and personal. After noticing a spike of electricity on a device designed to monitor electrical flow, an investigator inspected the area to debunk the activity. Electrical spikes don't necessarily mean a ghost is present, investigators say; it could just be faulty wiring or a surge of static electricity. But this investigator didn't get a chance to debunk the phenomena. As he walked under a set of stairs where the activity seemed to originate, he felt a hand pass through his hair.

All the evidence lends credence to the idea that the Cincinnati Observatory is an actual haunting—not an urban legend.

# Duke Chapel—Duke University

## *Duke's First Family of Haunting*

Duke University gets its name not from some far-off European royal ties, but from an American version of a royal family—the Duke family. It turns out that American royalty has just as much propensity to spawn ghost stories as their European counterparts.

George Washington Duke, a tobacco magnate, used his power to move Trinity College to Durham and continued to be the school's main benefactor. In 1924, the school became known as Duke University. George Duke, himself, along with sons, James and Benjamin, are entombed in the Memorial Chapel, a small chapel located near the imposing Duke Chapel. The chapel serves as a focal point for the campus, placed at both the center of the campus and on the highest ridge. It's one of the highest buildings in Durham County.

With the chapel's gothic-inspired architecture and its imposing pipe organ, the building looks—and sounds—haunted. Photographers have noticed a strange shadow that appears when they try to take a picture of the chapel under the right conditions. They call it the "ghost chapel." Is it a hint of ghostly presences within? Some students think so.

To bolster the stories of chapel ghosts, several other university dignitaries are buried on the chapel grounds.

Actually, the story of the George Duke's interments has taken a life, no pun intended, of its own. The story is that a group of workers showed up at the Duke family's private burial plot at 3 a.m. They had no idea what the job was. But they soon found out. Their job was to dig up the bodies of the George, James, and Benjamin and re-bury them at Memorial Chapel.

The Memorial Chapel is closed off to tourists.

Some people say that's because it's supposed to be a place of prayer and meditation. Other people say it's because the chapel and Memorial Chapel are haunted.

One story says that George Washington Duke didn't want to be interred in the Memorial Chapel and has manifested his displeasure by haunting the place. A medium, sitting on the grave, had a sudden impression that turned into a vision. She said she saw George Washington Duke dressed as Jesus Christ. He asked the medium to contact Duke heiress, Doris Duke, and "find the truth."

The medium said she was never allowed to relay the message. Maybe he's waiting for you to show up at Duke University to entrust you with his message.

The Duke family doesn't just haunt the campus. The family's haunted roots stretch out across the county.

Former Duke staff members who worked at the family home, located about five miles west of campus, told a newspaper writer that the Duke Homestead was also haunted.

An employee who had the unenviable task of working overnight said he saw a weird light glowing from inside the farmhouse. The worker could not figure out the source of the light. But that was nothing compared to the worker's next encounter with the ghost that haunted the property. Once, the worker saw a woman dressed in nineteenth-century clothing appear in the window.

I imagine it's hard to keep good help at the Duke Homestead.

## Rossborough Inn—University of Maryland
### *Temporary Guests, Permanent Ghosts*

The Rossborough Inn is one of the most famous spots on the University of Maryland's College Park campus. There are a few reasons for that.

First, it's the oldest building on campus. John Ross, a land speculator and tavern owner, built it between 1804 and 1812. The land and inn eventually was bought by two brothers, Charles Benedict Calvert and George Henry, who sold some land and the inn to the Maryland Agricultural College.

The inn also served as a temporary residence of some famous and infamous characters. Union General Ambrose E. Burnside camped out near the inn, and Confederate General Bradley T. Johnson made it his headquarters.

Sure, Burnside's men tore down a section of fence during their campus stay and Johnson's troops did more partying than fighting during their encampment, but like most decent guests, they went their way after their stay was finished.

But, you know how there are always those few guests who overstay their welcome? Well, at the Rossborough Inn, a few temporary guests have become permanent ghosts.

Larry Donnelly, a former dining services manager at the Rossborough Inn, said he met one of these eternal residents one morning.

It all started early one morning in 1981 when he had an office at the Rossborough. The inn was going through renovation work at the time. That's important to note because paranormal researchers believe that renovation work can lead to hauntings.

Donnelly probably wasn't aware of that, though, when a sudden gust of wind blew through an open window and grabbed his attention. He looked out the door and saw a woman smiling back at him. The way Donnelly described the woman, she sounded a lot like the ghost of Miss Betty, the manager of the inn during the Civil War and at least one of the spirits said to be haunting the Rossborough.

Another encounter with not one, but two apparitions was reported in the student newspaper, called the *Diamondback*. According to the paper, a paranormal specialist saw two spirits sitting on stools in the nearby Carriage House restaurant.

Not everyone needs a face-to-face meeting with one of the inn's ghosts to realize the place is haunted. A lot of folks have reported unusual activity and felt unseen presences in the building

Stephen Oetken, a dining services staff member, said, "You just never feel as if you are alone in that place."

He's been part of a couple incidents that have convinced him that this weird feeling is more than a typical case of the willies. Oetken said that once campus police called and said the alarm had been tripped. Nothing seemed amiss, until they checked out Oetken's office. The office had a corner window shaped like a half-moon. Much to Stephen's amazement, the window was wide open. The police suggested that a squirrel might have opened the window.

But, as Oetken pointed out, the door latched from the inside. That's one pretty smart, super-strong squirrel.

Whoever or whatever is haunting the Rossborough is a polite spirit. One story is that he, or she, or it, likes to decorate. Once, the story goes, a staff member was cleaning out the bathroom that was temporarily being used as a closet. She cleaned up and organized as much as possible and then locked the bathroom door.

The next morning, she called Stephen in a panic. Apparently the ghost had left a message. He went over to investigate for himself. There, sitting on the ledge in the bathroom, was a beautiful vase with a flower bud inside.

It wasn't there just a few hours before.

"I knew what every piece looked like in that inn and I can tell you I have never seen that vase before," Oetken said.

Other paranormal activity was documented by Deborah Koch, who, as a student, gathered stories for a Maryland Folklore Archives assignment back in the 1970s. Apparently the Rossborough has a door that opens all by itself and lights that inexplicably turn on and off without any human intervention.

The lights, like a lot of the apparitions and paranormal activity at the inn, are selective about acting up. The building has been used for a variety of university functions, both administrative and social. (It was once home of the Maryland Faculty and Alumni Club.) However, most people won't notice anything amiss during the day-to-day hustle and bustle.

You get the biggest scares when you're alone, reported one former manager of the Faculty Club.

# 9
# OFF-CAMPUS HAUNTS

## School Spirits Found in Off-Campus Locations

Paranormal events and supernatural forces don't stop at the walls and gates of the university. It seems that wherever the high spirits and hijinks associated with students go, the power to haunt soon follows.

This means that host communities and branch campuses have their own share of ghost lore.

Host communities are the towns and cities that spring up around the university. Students need housing, food, entertainment, clothes, and other services that these communities are happy—or at least willing—to provide. Those towns also provide students one more place to find ghosts, poltergeists, and other paranormal phenomena. Haunted bookstores, bars, restaurants, apartments, and graveyards are just a few of the supernatural hot spots you'll find in these communities.

Branch campuses are sometimes looked at as the little brothers or sisters of a university's main campus. Students may attend a branch campus instead of the main campus for a number of academic, financial, and geographic reasons.

But there's nothing little about the type of ghostly activity that goes on there.

In the upcoming pages, we'll discover the full range of haunted activity at these campuses. One campus built near both a sacred Native American spot and a graveyard is plagued with a range of activity—from a full-body apparition to poltergeist-like object throwing. There are also a few ghosts lurking in a mansion that was restored and used as an administration building.

We'll start our tour at one of the most haunted host towns, Iowa City.

## Ghostess with the Mostess and other Iowa City Ghost Stories

There's a lot of speculation why the University of Iowa is so haunted.

The best reason—the university is located smack dab in the middle of a really haunted city. Iowa City is one of the Midwest's most haunted locales. Students who think they can escape the ghosts and spirits of the campus find that the supernatural reaches into the buildings and stores of the host city. One of the most haunted spots is a seemingly innocent-looking bookstore.

A lot of Iowa students complain about the price of textbooks. There's just something deeply ironic and disturbing about paying over a hundred bucks for a slim volume on Finance, right?

But it's not prices that haunt students at the University of Iowa, it's an actual ghost that haunts them at the truly appropriately named Haunted Bookstore.

The ghost, who affectionately goes by the name of Claire, is a friendly sort of ghost. In fact, if reports are to be believed, it's so friendly that Claire should be placed on the payroll, or sign up for a work-study agreement. According to one legend, if a student needs something and asks for it out loud while shopping at the shop, Claire will make sure the student receives it.

Talk about financial aid.

And, students say this isn't just requests for additional 10 percent discount on paperbacks, they say Claire can deliver major requests, like a bookshop. The owner of the bookstore said that the money she used to buy the shop came when she asked "Claire" for help.

Wonder what the biggest student request is for Claire?

"Oh, Claire, let me graduate in four years!"

If you do make a trip to the bookstore (haunted or not) in Iowa City, you'll probably come across a few books that tell the story of the city's most famous otherworldly resident—the Black Angel. It's almost a graduation requirement for students to travel to the Oakland Cemetery, preferably at night, and pay tribute to a statue of an angel that rests above the field of silent grave markers.

As visitors gaze on what most folks call the Black Angel, the notice some strange things about the statue. First, it doesn't really have that serene, beatific look that's common among most angelic figures that adorn the graves at other graveyards. This has a menacing look. Some people say it's the Angel of Death.

Another weird trait of the Black Angel is that it appears to watch you, wherever you go in the cemetery. Talk about Hawkeyes.

The statue has spawned a whole series of legends and reported curses. One of the most famous cursed objects is the Black Angel of Oakland Cemetery.

They say everyone has an angel looking out for you. In Iowa, at least according to a spooky tale about a statue near the University of Iowa, they have an angel that's just looking to get you.

Because she looks more like the Angel of Death than the sweet, lute-playing guardian angel type, locals have dubbed her "The Black Angel." She watches over the Oakland Cemetery from her perch eight-and-a-half feet in the air. If posture is any indication, it's a task that she finds particularly burdensome. She crouches over the earthly remains of the Feldevert family with creepy eyes that visitors swear watch them— not matter where they are in the graveyard.

She does more than watch, though. People say she can reach out and touch you, if you're not careful.

You could ask Ali Garaets, who lived in the shadow of the Black Angel for years, and told her own encounter story in *Weird Hauntings*.

It happened back in 2000. Ali and a bunch of friends were at a backyard bonfire. She was just 16. And, just as teenagers often do during parties, they began to discuss scary stories and urban legends. It didn't take long before the Black Angel came up.

They started to discuss the legend. Anyone who defaced the monument usually paid dearly. There were all sorts of stories about kids who didn't heed this warning. For instance, a couple of kids supposedly urinated on the monument one night. Later that night, they were all killed in a car crash. Which just goes to show you, never get in a pissing match with the ghost of a graveyard monument.

Ali's friends were undeterred. At 2 a.m., the intrepid foursome drove down Prairie du Chien Road toward Hickory Hill Park. From there, they climbed the lonely hill to Oakland Cemetery. The graveyard was absolutely still. Time seems to stand still during supernatural encounters, and Garaets said she lost track of time as the crew journeyed through the cemetery to find the Black Angel.

Suddenly, though, she was right in front of her, towering against the moonlit sky.

There was quite a debate as to what to do next. Each teen dared the other to touch the angel.

Finally, one brave—or stupid—boy reached out and touched the base of the statue.

They looked up.

An ethereal, silver halo formed around the head of the angel. That was enough to freak out the amateur ghost hunters, but what really scared them was the angel's glowing eyes.

As she reported, "They were silver in the moonlight, but not because of the reflections from the moon. She looked positively demonic."

So what did Ali Garaets and her brave friends do? They ran. They bolted through the cemetery, toward the wall.

As they did, Ali swore she heard piercing screams chase them from the interior of the graveyard. It wasn't the wind. They were sure of that.

Years later, Garaets did return to the cemetery. Of course, she visited during normal hours and there were no dares or jokes. She brought fresh flowers and left them at the grave of the Feldevert family, resting under the watchful gaze of the Black Angel.

Her advice: "If you go to see the Black Angel, be respectful and understand she's watching over the entire cemetery."

If you do visit the site, you may also notice a few missing digits on the statue. There's another story that emphasizes Ali's advice.

Apparently, some young man used a hacksaw to take a thumb off the statue. Later, he was found in the Chicago River. The coroner ruled his death from strangulation and a blackened thumbprint was found on his neck. A few days later, the caretaker found a bronze thumb resting serenely on the base of the monument.

A popular time for University of Iowa stories and visits to the statue is Halloween, of course. But it may not be the best idea. A legend states that on Halloween the angel statue gets darker and more ominous. Reportedly, one statue of a small girl glows at night and, often, student photographers find strange "orbs" dotting their pictures of the statue. Parapsychologists say these orbs are actually a version of spirit photography.

Huge thumbprints that appear on pictures, however, may just be a sign of bad photography.

# McCall Hall—University of Minnesota-Crookston
## The Haunted Branches

The University of Minnesota's main campus seems to get all the attention. Located in the heart of Minneapolis-St. Paul, it serves as a hub of music and the arts. Students also have ready access to a vibrant downtown nightlife, shopping, major sporting events, and other amenities that are only found in a big city.

But it's not for everyone.

Some students decide to attend a branch campus. One advantage of the branch campus is they have access to great educational opportunities without the big-city expenses and hassles. They also have access to the same paranormal opportunities, apparently.

One haunted campus is the University of Minnesota-Crookston, a crown jewel in the system located in rural northwestern Minnesota. It was once the Northwest School of Agriculture and officially became a coordinate campus in 1969. The college was re-named the University of Minnesota-Crookston in 1988.

McCall Hall is one of the school's residence halls. Built in 1946, it was named after a T. M. McCall, pioneer in agricultural science, and, over the years, established a reputation as being haunted.

Residents often complain about strange voices echoing through the building at odd hours. When they investigate, they can't locate the source. The stories turn stranger. A few witnesses have spotted a full-body apparition.

Who this stranger is and why the spirit haunts this unlikely haunted building is a matter of intense speculation from UM-Crookston students.

Whether or not this is an actual haunted location or not, it must beef up ticket sales for the Halloween haunted house held in the basement of McCall Hall.

# Haunted Branch Campuses—
# University of Pittsburgh
## *Community Campuses with Paranormal Problems of Their Own*

The University of Pittsburgh is known for its urban center in the steel city. But it's far more than that.

Years ago, university administrators decided to take the wonders of a Pitt education across Pennsylvania. Small communities whose young residents were not able to attend the university suddenly had a Pitt campus in their backyard.

Besides immersing these branch campuses in Pitt traditions, the university apparently exported its biggest tradition—good ghost stories.

### GREENSBURG

The quaint community of Greensburg has a long history that follows the nation's development. The town, situated just southeast of Pittsburgh, was named after Revolutionary War hero Nathanael Greene. The community matured during the Industrial Revolution, becoming a vital transportation and mining link for the growing manufacturing and industrial center of Pittsburgh.

Greensburg's place in history is well known. Its place as a center for paranormal history is even more established.

Hidden in the woods of the Allegheny Mountains, the small town of Kecksburg is close to Greensburg. The town is world famous in paranormal circles as the site of a reported UFO crash. The story goes that on December 9, 1965, a strange object streaked across the sky above Kecksburg, glanced off the treetops, and crashed into the woods outside of town.

The crash attracted onlookers and, ominously, members of the law enforcement community and the military. Some witnesses, before they were rushed off the crash site by soldiers, said they saw a craft that resembled an acorn smoldering in the middle of the woods.

Military and government officials produced a range of explanations for the night's events. The crash was nothing more than fragments of a meteorite, or a piece of a Russian satellite that reentered the earth's atmosphere.

The witnesses and other experts on the case who don't buy the military's explanation say that Kecksburg, like Roswell, is part of a massive government cover-up.

Ever since the Kecksburg crash, the Greensburg area was placed on the map for paranormal adventurers who visit Roswell, Area 51, and Gulf Breeze. In fact, Kecksburg has been referred to as "Pennsylvania's Roswell."

But, as the lengthy lore about the University of Pittsburgh at Greensburg will demonstrate, UFOs aren't the only paranormal phenomena that you'll encounter in a visit to this corner of Pennsylvania, especially when you tour this jewel in the crown of Pitt's campus system.

The UP-Greensburg campus is haunted, really haunted, students report. Campus stories pinpoint one building in particular as the most haunted on campus—Lynch Hall.

Lynch Hall was a grand tudor mansion that belonged to Commander Charles McKenna Lynch. The Commander was an executive for the H. C. Frick Coke Company, which had a number of facilities in the Greensburg area.

According to a story in the *Pittsburgh Tribune Review*, Charles graduated from the U.S. Naval Academy. That's the most likely reason why people nicknamed him "Commander." Besides being a war hero, he became a community leader, heading banking and brokerage businesses. He was even the president of the Pittsburgh Stock Exchange.

Constructed in 1923, the Commander's mansion rested on an impressive estate. It was dubbed—nautically—the Starboard Light.

In 1963, the Commander died and the mansion eventually passed into the hands of the University of Pittsburgh. The mansion actually became the centerpiece for the nascent Greensburg campus, serving as a functional administration building—and a postcard backdrop for the budding campus.

But it wasn't just the architecture that had students and visitors talking about Lynch Hall. It wasn't the aesthetics. It wasn't even the vast interior that gave UP-Greensburg plenty of room to expand. It was Lynch Hall's ghost—or, depending on whom you talk to, maybe even ghosts.

It seemed like as soon as Pitt officials started to renovate the building, stories began to surface that the mansion had an unexpected resident on the premises.

At first, the tales were brushed off as overactive imaginations. Indeed, in the right light (or the right darkness, to be more precise), Lynch Hall and its sharp angles and pointed towers are textbook haunted house material.

But it was more than just the appearance that was a little unsettling. Despite laughing off the first reports of haunted activity, more official reports began to seep in. The stories of ghostly encounters didn't come from a few inebriated college kids or a couple of visitors caught up in the intimidating size and solemn history of Lynch Hall—these reports came from some of the most respected and well-trained observers in the University of Pitt system—university guards.

Security guards who have the unenviable task of watching over Lynch Hall in the depths of night were among the first campus officials to acknowledge the paranormal presence in the building.

Guards reported that once night fell and darkness invaded the mansion, the building filled with strange sights and sounds. Guards even reported running into a filmy, but unmistakable human presence while making their rounds in the mansion. They swore it was the ghost of Commander Lynch.

The stories of encounters with the Commander's ghost spread. It even reached the heirs of the Commander. When his great-grandchildren took a tour of Lynch Hall, the family made sure they inquired about the hall's haunted presence. The security guard obliged with a slew of stories that detailed strange run-ins and incidents at Lynch Hall.

Most sightings happen in the area that used to be the Commander's office, the officers told the family. This section contains the office, two bedrooms, and a spiral staircase.

In one instance, the guard said that during the nightly rounds she went into the second-floor bathroom to close and lock a window. As she exited, she was shocked to see movement in the room's bathtub. A sad-eyed man sat in the tub, his knees clenched into his body. The man never spoke, but "telepathically" conveyed a question to the frightened guard: "What are you doing in my bathroom?"

The guard, not believing her own eyes, quickly looked away and then looked again, hoping that when she turned her head again the apparition would have turned out to be a figment of her imagination.

No such luck.

He was still there.

She ran to get another guard. When they came back, the man was gone, but the guards were speechless when they saw that the window was open again and the bathroom door appeared to also be cracked open.

The ghost was not quite finished with this intrepid guard. She said in another instance, she walked to the main door of Lynch Hall and saw a figure at the top of the stairs. He was leaning on the railing and was dressed in the clothes of an earlier period.

He said, "Well, are you coming in?" to the guard.

She didn't accept the invitation. Although she said she didn't feel threatened, she refused to go in.

The Commander didn't just appear to people in uniform. One workman reported to the guards that he saw a man in a blue dress uniform. It was an apt description of a uniform a U.S. Naval officer or a graduate of the U.S. Naval Academy would have worn. The guards were not surprised. They knew exactly who the sailor was.

Finally, a psychic had been called in to offer her impressions of the building. As soon as she entered the hall, she was floored by the supernatural vibrations. She reported to others that she felt the presence of a male spirit. Without any apparent prior knowledge of the building's haunted history, the psychic correctly repeated details of the encounter with the ghost in the bathroom. The psychic reassured the guards that the ghost was not evil—he was actually being playful.

The members of the Lynch family and others who knew the Commander are split about who the source of the haunting is. One side of the family says this doesn't sound like the Commander, who was not much of a prankster. They also believe the former naval officer would identify himself.

However, others in the family say the apparition seen in Lynch Hall is without question Commander Lynch. During tours, one great-grandchild of the Commander felt—and perhaps saw—a presence in the section that is reportedly the hub of this haunting. The descendant detailed the encounter on a message board:

"I could feel something in one of the bedrooms and it made me catch my breath and my eyes water. I could feel something or someone was there. I was face to face with him, but could not see him. Although, I did see some motion in the air. It had kind of a fluid look, and I'm sure it wasn't my eyes."

"I simply said, 'Why are you here Great Grandfather, you need to go on?' Then I left the room to catch my breath. I know someone or something is in that house. I would like to help him make his peace with God."

Another question people ask is: Why is Lynch Hall haunted?

The Commander lived a contented life, it seems. Not to say that hauntings are always caused by sad moments, but tales of misfortune often linger behind haunted legends. Oddly, tragedy doesn't seem to be especially affixed to Lynch Hall as it is in other reputed haunted homes. No suicides or murders or accidental deaths appear to have occurred at Lynch Hall.

There is one interesting speculation.

They say the activity is caused by renovations to the mansion. Renovation work is actually a frequently cited reason for homes that were once supernaturally quiet to suddenly burst into paranormal activity.

The renovations to Lynch Hall—which even the living seem to complain about—may have stirred the Commander's activity. Maybe he is upset that his sanctuary has been disturbed.

Or he just doesn't like the new decor.

And that's all you need: the ghost of a naval officer who thinks he's an interior decorator.

## Spirit Communications 101: G-E-T- O-U-T

In 2008, a group of brave University of Pittsburgh-Greensburg students decided to take the spirit matters of Lynch Hall into their own hands. Led by two resident advisors and armed with candles and a Ouija board, about 35 students struck off to the basement of the infamous hall to see if they could communicate with the phantom full-time naval officer, part-time interior decoration critic.

The article, which appeared in the *Pittsburgh Tribune-Review*, detailed the adventure. Before the investigation, the RAs made sure to prime the student spirit-seekers with a brief talk about Charles McKenna Lynch and offered full disclosure of the ghost sightings in the building, especially the story about the campus police officer who refuses to work the night shift at Lynch Hall. After a brief glimpse of Lynch's portrait (so the students could identify the ghost), the group was ready for the séance.

With the Ouija board set on the floor and two candles flickering in the dark, the students began to ask the spirits—if there were any in the premises—questions. As the pointer, called a planchette, drifted along the board and appeared to be guided toward a jumble of letters on the board, some more definite answers came through.

When the students asked if Lynch was present, the word "YES" was spelled out.

Things were about to get creepier.

As the séance continued, the sound of water began to echo in the basement. While students assumed a guard had flushed the toilet in one of the floors above them, the sound continued...and continued.

As far as they knew, no one else was in the building.

The students asked the Ouija board if the Commander was responsible for the sounds. Again, the board replied: "YES."

The next message was even more disturbing. When the students asked if the spirit wanted them to leave, the reply, "G-E-T O-U-T," was methodically spelled out.

About half the group accepted the spirit's invitation and bolted for the Lynch Hall door.

Natalie Czmola, one of the students who attended the outing told the reporter, "The fact it said, 'Get out,' I'm not comfortable with that. It creeps me out, but it's interesting."

Not everyone ducked out at the first indication of supernatural conflict. A group of students continued to ask questions and the spirit grew more agitated.

When the students asked if the spirit had something to tell the world, the word "HELP" was spelled out. The pointer slid across the board to the "yes" mark when the group asked if the spirit was trapped on earth and then spelled out "DEATH."

The spirit had one more message for the students who asked if the spirit planned to visit any other campus buildings that night. "RS" was the reply.

Did the spirit just spell out the initials of the Robertshaw dorm— the home of most of these spirit-seeking students?

Whether the spirit really did move the planchette to communicate with the students, or the subconscious desires of the Ouija board operators directed the answers, it's a good bet that students who attended the Lynch Hall séance that night slept a little less soundly at Robertshaw.

## JOHNSTOWN

Johnstown, a city of 26,000 people that rests about 60 miles east of Pittsburgh, is host to University of Pitt at Johnstown. It's also host to its share of restless spirits.

The city of Johnstown is one of the few places that managed to turn a disaster into a tourist attraction.

Johnstown sits, like a bucket, in a valley completely surrounded by towering mountains. In 1889, the city paid dearly for this topographical anomaly.

During a spell of heavy May rains in 1889, the nearby South Fork Dam collapsed. A wall of water, picking up trees, houses, train cars, metal, and other debris, followed the natural contours of the earth and crashed headlong into the city. The flood and fires that followed killed thousands of citizens and spawned dozens of legends about spirits and ghosts around Johnstown.

The South Fork dam is a spiritual epicenter.

Another favorite haunt in the Johnstown area is the Stone Bridge. According to historical accounts, a 30-foot pile of debris jammed up against the Stone Bridge beneath the South Fork Dam.

When the bridge eventually broke, the rush of water—picking up trees, pieces of homes, train cars, and barbed wire—rushed into the valley like a tsunami from Hell. To complete the hellish effect, the oil that spilled into the flooding waters caught on fire.

The bodies were washed away. Some were never recovered. But residents also say that their souls continue to live on. There are even reports of desperate cries of "help" cascading down the valley from the infamous spot of the Stone Bridge.

If the story of that 1889 flood was one of Pennsylvania's most tragic tales, accounts of how Johnstown rebuilt was one the state's most heroic moments. Not only did the town rebuild, but the flood recovery effort became a rallying point for the city's resourcefulness and hardiness—a legacy that helped them through future upheavals, like the loss of the steel and coal industries. The Johnstown area even created a tourist industry out of the event, attracting thousands of tourists each year who are interested in seeing the site of the Great Flood, visiting the Flood Museum, and catching sight of some ghosts that haunt the city.

A dramatic example of Johnstown's ability to survive disaster and reinvent itself is the campus of the University of Pitt-Johnstown. The campus, established in Johnstown in 1927, was one of the first examples of a regional campus.

In the early 1960s, the campus was moved to Richland Township, a part of Johnstown that would give the school more room to grow. By 1967, the campus included two classroom buildings, dormitories, and a student union. Over the years, it's grown considerably. And so have reports of paranormal encounters.

The Pitt campus at Johnstown reflects the town's spooky tradition and may even rival its big brother campus in Pittsburgh, at least in the number of rumored hauntings and supernatural activity.

Strangely, few of the UP-Johnstown ghosts are apparently connected with the floods. Students claim that the eerie happenings at the school are caused by the site's unique location.

The campus, they say, is built on sacred ground.

Legend has it that the campus rests on ground that indigenous people considered sacred and that Native American graves were disturbed during the construction of several campus buildings.

This is a paranormal no-no.

There's evidence that lends credence to this theory. Shawnee and Delaware tribes were active in western Pennsylvania and had settlements near Johnstown. Experts of these indigenous cultures have identified burial mounds in the region, as well. (The mound at a nearby site, called Fort Hill, is perhaps the most famous example of an area burial mound.)

Campus paranormal theorists say there were Indian mounds on campus. But these mounds were removed to make way for the Johnstown branch.

If it is true, it could explain the paranormal activity on the school's athletic fields. For most colleges, a rowdy, cheering student section creates a home field advantage, called school spirit. UP-Johnstown takes it one step beyond, bolstering school spirit with actual spirits.

The soccer field has earned a particular reputation for being haunted by the ghosts of Native Americans. Students claim to hear weird noises that drift in the wind over the fields and feel unseen presences on the athletic fields.

There are those who say, if you listen closely, you'll realize that the noise isn't a noise at all. It's the sound of Native American spirits singing. Perhaps it's just residual energy of the tribes that's trapped on the campus. Or maybe these voices are raising songs of lament, crying for the land they once owned.

Those eerie melodies of the area's first inhabitants—and perhaps their spirits—drift off the athletic fields and into some of the nearby buildings, too, students report.

Oak Hall and Laurel Hall, which are nestled in these reportedly haunted woods, are the sites of several campus ghost tales. The dorms, like the athletic field, are supposedly built directly on sacred territory.

During the night, people claim to hear drumming erupting from the woods that surround the dorms. And, to the best of the students' collective knowledge, the marching band doesn't practice in the wee hours of the morning. Most say this is the drumming of the native spirits displaced by the campus construction.

Only the brave walk across that sliver of land that separates the dorms at night when this ghostly drumming is heard.

But even the solid walls of the dorm form no protection against these restless spirits. Paranormal activity has been reported in both buildings. Apparitions have been spotted in the residence halls and objects have been seen moving all by themselves.

The incidents occurred so frequently—and became so creepy—that at least one group of students banded together to rid their temporary homes of their permanent otherworldly residences. (After all, they weren't chipping in on food and utilities.) Using common ghostbusting techniques, they tried to exorcise the ghost—or ghosts—in the dorm.

The process is also called a banishment, and the success rate of the operation is difficult to nail down. How successful this student-led exorcism was is also a matter of debate.

Right after the ceremony, students claim that far from ridding the room of its paranormal roommate, the activity increased and became more dangerous. Instead of harmless objects moving slightly, sharp objects flew across the room.

On the other hand, there have been fewer and fewer tales of haunting in these dorms over the past decade or so.

Maybe it just took time for the effects of the banishment to settle in. Or maybe the spirits just took an off-campus apartment?

## THE HAUNTED CEMETERY

There are other spectral suspects said to haunt the grounds of Pitt's Johnstown campus.

The ghost of a small girl has been spotted walking through the campus and drifting in several dorm rooms. In one story, a group of students said they took a walk along the nature trail at UP-Johnstown. The students watched as a small girl walked the trail just in front of them.

The girl seemed to recognize the presence of the students, but continued to walk. She disappeared around a turn in the path.

Intrigued, the students assumed the girl, who was too small and too young to be a college student, was visiting her older college-age sibling. But there was something unsettling about the brief encounter. First, her dress was practically antique, not like anything girls wear today. Another thing caught the group off guard—she had a "filmy" appearance.

Intrigue transformed to fear. After all, they knew the rumors that the ghost of a girl haunts the campus. She is buried just up the path in the small cemetery that borders the southern edge the UP-Johnstown campus, right behind the paranormally active athletic fields.

When the students made the turn in the trail, hoping to see a real-live human girl still walking ahead of them, they saw nothing. The girl had vanished.

The students wondered: Did they just see the ghost of the UP-Johnstown cemetery?

According to a *Johnstown Tribune-Democrat* story, the university bought a 360-acre piece of land that included the cemetery back in 1966. There's no indication, however, when the ghost of the girl began to show up in campus's lengthy haunted lore.

But the theory of the ghost girl is borne out by research done by the area's genealogists and historians. The cemetery is sometimes referred to as Baumgardner Cemetery. The Baumgardner family lived on the plot years before the university purchased the land near the graveyard. Ruins of the old farm can still be seen near the plot of land.

The cemetery contains about 85 graves—many unmarked or barely marked—and is one of the largest private cemeteries in Richland Township. The strangest markers are called Fieldstones. For the plain, hard-working farmers, ornate headstones were rare. The families, instead, marked flat rocks with initials of the deceased and the dates of their death.

It's easy to see why a cemetery so close to campus would inspire a ghost story or two among the students. After all, based on the hundreds of other college ghost stories, placing a cemetery on or near a university campus is going to increase the probability of a few campus legends cropping up. But the details of the ghost stories at this cemetery are different. These details convince paranormal experts that there's something more to the tales than the typical overactive collegiate imagination.

One example: Most of the witnesses say they see a young girl. She's dressed in clothes of an earlier time period, often believed to be late-nineteenth-century or early twentieth-century garb.

The cemetery would contain graves of people who died during that exact period.

Here's where things get eerie. According to the genealogical study, the remains of several children lie in the quiet cemetery. And, several of these children were girls of the age described by the witnesses. Markers testify to this tragic loss of young lives. One stone etched in letters now dulled and faded by time lists several children and infants who died before their full flower of life.

Another stone reads "Children of M & E Baumgardner." The third stone segment reads "Loved In Life," then "In Death Remembered."

These stone markers are perhaps the most substantial manifestation of the sorrow felt for innocent lives that were cut far too short.

But could there be other manifestations of the emotion and grief that surrounds the death of a child? Could the apparition of the girl seen strolling along the nature trail be a marker of a different sort? Could it be that UP-Johnstown students walking along the nature trail have somehow stumbled onto a spiritual echo of the past?

The ghost may yet remind us of one more thing: there is a whole world to explore just outside of the laboratories and classrooms that make up one of Pitt's most haunted branch campuses.

The previous stories are the best-known and better-documented legends of Johnstown. But, there are others.

Wrapped in whispers and rumors, other buildings at UP-Johnstown land on the campus's "also haunted" list. The Living/Learning Center, a thoroughly modern residence unit, is one of those places. It seems to be an unlikely spot to catch a sighting of a ghost. The facility was constructed in 1994 and features modern conveniences. That's pretty modern to build a haunted history.

But, according to a few reports that have filtered in, apparitions have been seen in the building. Spectral noises have been heard, as well. *The Complete Idiot's Guide to Ghosts and Hauntings* reports that there are a number of ghosts there, including the ghost of a boy and a woman.

More distressing for students who like to sleep in, there are even tales of the ghost of an old man who screams at students when they're asleep.

Wonder if he has a snooze button for those 8 a.m. classes?

## *Afterword*

# Are Universities Really Haunted?

When I first started collecting and examining stories about the collegiate paranormal, I was quite skeptical as to the veracity of the accounts.

There was such a large number of these campus ghost stories that I didn't want to paint them all with such a broad brush, but, to me and my natural journalistic skepticism, the stories of campus ghosts and poltergeists could be explained by natural phenomena. More importantly, I felt the unique student culture played a major role in the creation and preservation of ghost stories.

At some of the universities examined in this volume, the student population is in the tens of thousands. It's what we call a "migratory population." That means that each year, as one class graduates and spreads the university's tales and legends to the world outside of the campus gates, there are also thousands of new students who must learn the history of their school and the culture of its student body. This is no easy task.

One way that culture and history is passed on most effectively is through verbal traditions, i.e., stories.

Ghost stories on campus, then, play an important role in preserving legends and transferring the cultural cues onto succeeding classes. As an example, the story of Old Coaly, Penn State's ghost mule, seems like a frivolous, fun tale. And there doesn't seem to be firsthand accounts of meeting up with the animal's ghost—sober accounts, at least. But, what the story does accurately pass on is Penn State's rich agricultural, blue collar origins. That simple tale confers more about the hard-working nature of Penn State students than pages out of the school's official history.

Likewise, think about the story of the Gipper's ghost at Notre Dame. It's more than just a tale of haunted hijinks—it's an enshrinement of one of the university's most sacred gridiron legends.

But are there actually dead mules and a football player on horseback trotting around America's biggest campuses? That's doubtful.

There's another reason to question whether paranormal forces have anything to do with the accounts of ghosts and spirits on campus. Most major universities are more than a century old. Some buildings that still serve core functions on these campuses are just as old. As any homeowner who has a century-plus house will tell you, old buildings creak and settle. Doors can appear to shut on their own. In fact, a whole range of paranormal phenomena can be mimicked by nothing more than excessive wear and tear of a building.

At this point, we're probably willing to dismiss all of the campus ghost stories as a form of college entertainment—good stories to be told around the dorm on stormy, autumn nights.

However, we shouldn't be too hasty to label all of these tales as campus legends. After spending more than a decade collecting these tales and, especially after publishing my first volume of university ghost stories, I have talked with numerous witnesses and paranormal researchers and have read the accounts of literally hundreds of people who have had experiences that have to be described as bizarre, at the least. The folks I talked to are sober, well-spoken, and well-meaning people who make excellent witnesses. Their accounts have a weird juxtaposition, both totally supernatural and entirely believable. In a twist on Occam's razor, the natural explanations that I tried to raise to explain the stories are less believable and more complex than paranormal explanations.

Paranormal researchers and ghost hunters have pointed out to me that some of the same reasons that make colleges and universities likely targets of fictional campus legends can be powerful paranormal forces.

For instance, old buildings don't just creak and moan. According to paranormal researchers, these structures have absorbed decades of psychic energy. This energy includes the positive, life-affirming power of students eager to embrace a new life, as well as negative energy radiating from misfortune and tragedy. The end result, these researchers say, are sites with a high potential for haunting.

Similarly, the natural tendency for university students to believe in campus legends may actually make them susceptible to paranormal encounters. Consciousness and belief play integral roles in the supernatural. Researchers say that paranormal run-ins are better described as a relationship that builds between the real and supernatural worlds, rather than a simple one-way encounter where a witness stumbles onto a ghost or some other type of anomalous event. If this is the case, the zealous capacity for college students to believe, which cynics might label as naïve, would feed into this spirit-making process.

Whether you believe that there are supernatural forces at work on the campuses of America's institutions of higher learning or merely think that the only spirits are located at the nearby university watering hole, I hope this volume has given you a chance to look at both sides of this interesting debate.

After all, what would a university be without powerful and passionate debate?

# Bibliography

## *Indiana University*

Walsh, Tony. "Ghoulish IU Tales Permeate Union, Spook Local Cemetery," *Indiana Daily Student*, October 30, 2009. http://www.idsnews.com/news/story.aspx?id=71512&search=haunted&section=search.

## *University of Iowa*

Austin, Joanne, ed. *Weird Hauntings, True Tales of Haunted Places.* New York: Sterling, 2010.

Trollinger, Vernon. *Haunted Iowa City.* Charleston, SC: The History Press, 2011.

## *The University of Minnesota*

Downer, Deborah. *Classic American Ghost Stories.* Little Rock, AR: August House Publishers, 1990.

*The Minnesota Daily.* Student newspaper of the University of Minnesota.

## University of Alabama

Barefoot, Daniel W. *Haunted Halls of Ivy: Ghosts of Southern Colleges and Universities.* Winston-Salem, NC: John F. Blair, 2004.

Della Costa, Anna Maria. "Do You Believe in Ghosts?" *Tuscaloosa News,* July 30, 2007. http://www.tuscaloosanews.com /article/20070930/NEWS/709300306.

Tuscaloosa Paranormal Research Group. "Kilgore House (University of Alabama)." http://www.tuscaloosaparanormal.com/index .php?option=com_content&view=article&id=124&Itemid=58.

Wright, Robin. "The University of Alabama." *Real Haunts.* http:// www.realhaunts.com/united-states/the-university-of-alabama/

Cobb, Mark Hughes. "Who Haunts the Halls of Tuscaloosa?" *Tuscaloosa News,* October 25, 2009. http://www.tuscaloosanews.com /article/20091025/NEWS/910239926.

Stevenson, Tommy. "Tour of Local Haunts." *Tuscaloosa News,* October 28, 2008. http://www.tuscaloosanews.com/article/20081028 /NEWS/810270224?p=1&tc=pg.

## University of Tennessee

*Tennessee Today.* http://www.utk.edu/tntoday/media/MorganHall Ghosts.xml

Shearer, John. "Last Day of Use as a Women's Dorm is at Hand for Historic UT Building." *Knoxville News Sentinel,* May 8, 2008. http://www.knoxnews.com/news/2008/may/08 /a-strong-sense-of-place/

Coleman, Christopher K. *Ghosts and Haunts of Tennessee.* Winston-Salem, NC: John F. Blair, 2011.

May, Melissa. "Resident Ghosts Haunt Three University Buildings." *University of Tennessee Daily Beacon,* October 27, 2004.

http://utdailybeacon.com/news/2004/oct/27/resident-ghosts-haunt-three-university-buildings/

Eastern Tennessee Paranormal Research Society case report on Strong Hall investigation. http://www.etprs.com/index.php?option=com_content&view=article&id=69:academic-ut-strong-hall&catid=38:locations&Itemid=96.

## University of Maryland

University Communications Newsdesk, University of Maryland. "Haunted Maryland: The Rossborough Inn." news release 2008. http://newsdesk.umd.edu/culture/2008/Halloween/Rossborough.cfm.

Ricksecker, Mike. *Ghosts of Maryland.* Altgen, PA: Schiffer Publishing, 2010.

———"Haunted Maryland," http://www.newsdesk.umd.edu/culture/2004/Halloween.cfm.

———"Haunted Maryland—2006." http://www.newsdesk.umd.edu/culture/release.cfm?ArticleID=1320.

*The Diamondback* Student newspaper of the University of Maryland.

"Maryland's Haunted Colleges." *Southern Maryland Online.* http://somd.com/news/headlines/2007/6631.shtml.

## Duke University

Weston, Victoria. "Rhine Center Researches Paranormal." *The Duke Chronicle*, October 31, 2005. http://dukechronicle.com/article/rhine-center-researches-paranormal.

"Duke Ghost Stories: Fact of Fiction?" *The Duke Chronicle*, October 23, 2003. http://dukechronicle.com/article/duke-ghost-stories-fact-or-fiction.

Padget, Angie. "Campus, Durham Ghost Legends Liven Local Lore." *The Duke Chronicle*, October 31, 2005. http://dukechronicle.com/article/campus-durham-ghost-legends-liven-local-lore.

Croft, Tara. "Specters Spook Campus." *Technician Online*, May 29, 2007. http://www.technicianonline.com/features /specters-spook-campus-1.1106607.

Evans, Jennifer. "Paranormal Investigators Search for Haunting Evidence." *Technician Online*, October 29, 2008. http://www .technicianonline.com/features/paranormal-investigators-search -for-haunting-evidence-1.852346.

## Boston College

"Boston and Salem Witch Hangings." *Massachusetts Travel Journal.* http://masstraveljournal.com/places/north-boston /boston-salem-witch-hangings.

Gawlik, Steven. "Stepping Inside Boston College's Legendary House of Mystery." *The Boston College Chronicle*, October 31, 2002. http:// www.bc.edu/bc_org/rvp/pubaf/chronicle/v11/o31/oconnell.html.

## Harvard University

Hoffenberg, Mark R. "I Saw a Ghost in my Common Room." *The Harvard Crimson*, November 9, 1985. http://www.thecrimson.com /article/1985/11/9/i-saw-a-ghost-in-my/

Ripich, Amy N. "Fearsom Phantoms Lurking in the Ivy." *The Harvard Crimson*, October 31, 1986. http://www.thecrimson.com /article/1986/10/31/fearsome-phantoms-lurking-in-the-ivy/

Savdie, Nicole. "Thayer and Its Friendly Ghost," *The Harvard Crimson*, October 29, 2009. http://www.thecrimson.com/article/2009/10/29 /ghosts-thayer-up-nbsp/

Bennett, Drake P. "Twilight Zone: The College Years." *The Harvard Crimson*, November 20, 1997. http://www.thecrimson.com /article/1997/11/20/twilight-zone-the-college-years-pcotton/

"The Nicest Building in the Yard." *Harvard Magazine*, Nov.-Dec., 2001. http://harvardmagazine.com/2001/11/the-nicest-building -in-t.html.

## Cornell

*Cornell Alumni Magazine*

Earle, Corey. *The Cornell Daily Sun*, October 25, 2006. http://cornell dailysun.com/node/19168.

Crane, Elaine Formam. *Killed Strangely: The Death of Rebecca Cornell.* Ithaca, NY: Cornell University Press, 2002.

Li, Lucy. "Violent History Belies Ithaca's Peaceful Aura," *The Cornell Daily Sun*, November 17, 2009. http://cornellsun. com/section/news/content/2009/11/17violent-history-belies-ithaca%E2%80%99s-peaceful-aura.

## University of Arizona

University of Arizona Mystery's. http://uofamystery.com/Hauntingof .htm.

Tafoya, Nathan. "Myth or Reality? Ghosts at the UA?" *Arizona Daily Wildcat*, October 31, 2003. http://wc.arizona.edu /papers/97/49/04_1.html.

http://www.metacafe.com/watch/2739251/ghost_appearance_at _university_of_arizona/

"Ghosts of the Prairie," http://www.prairieghosts.com/tucson.html.

## University of Oregon

Tammik, Ott. "A Supernatural Soirée." *Daily Oregon Emerald*, October 29, 2009. http://dailyemerald.com/2009/10/29 /a-supernatural-soiree/

## Iowa State

Lonsdale, John. "Haunting Discoveries." *Iowa State Daily*, October 29, 2009. http://www.iowastatedaily.com/news/article_1d72e2db -d152-5ea9-a4f0-f2ae6896c341.html.

Molitor, Amanda. "The Ghosts of Campus." *Iowa State Daily*, October 18, 2007. http://www.iowastatedaily.com/article_b9316b9c-2dee -5527-adeb-02a83a1b791e.html.

Payne, Erin. "ISU Has Plenty of Ghost Stories to Tell." *Iowa State Daily*, October 31, 1995. http://www.iowastatedaily.com/article _b84669d6-0ae9-5554-b46d-9d9092813b1e.html.

Layton, Arianna. "Don't Worry, It's a Nice Ghost." *Iowa State Daily*, October 31, 1996. http://www.iowastatedaily.com /article_2a64542b-4588-5efc-b608-4143e172da3f.html.

Calef, Zach. "Football Phantoms." *Iowa State Daily*, October 24, 2000. http://www.iowastatedaily.com/news/article_0a8ce0c4-7bfe-5c06 -a0eb-589941d93f0b.html.

### Kansas State

Urban, Rachel. "Legendary Ghost Still Spooks Theater." *Kansas State Collegian*, July 27, 2010. http://www.kstatecollegian.com/news /legendary-ghost-still-spooks-theater-1.2282579.

### University of Pittsburgh

Swayne, Matt. *Paranormal Pitt.* Createspace, 2008.

### University of Cincinnati

Spiritual Hope Society. "Case review and Evidence."http://www .spiritualhopesociety.com/Case_Review_and_Evidence.php.

*University of Cincinnati Horizons Magazine*

*Insider's Guide to the University of Cincinnati*

Moran, Mary Kate. "Ghost in the Stacks?" *The News Record*, October 26, 2005. http://www.newsrecord.org/index.php/article/2005/10 /ghost_in_the_stacksbr_

"Parkview Cornerstone of Cincinnati," *The News Record*, October 26, 2005. http://www.newsrecord.org/article/2004/07/ parkview_cornerstone_of_cincinnatibr_

Ando, Gin A. "The Zen of Greg Hand." *The News Record*,
   April 27, 2011. http://www.newsrecord.org/article/2011/04/
   the_zen_of_greg_handbr_

## *Georgetown University*

Alexander, Sheridan. "Hauntings at Georgetown University's
   Healy Hall: Washington DC Ghost Stories and Haunted Places."
   *Examiner.com*, October 1, 2009. http://www.examiner.com/article/
   hauntings-at-georgetown-university-s-healy-hall-washington-dc
   -ghost-stories-and-haunted-places.
Griesedieck, Lizzie. "For 30M: A Local Mansion. The Catch? May
   Coome with Ghosts." *The Hoya*, September 15, 2008. http://www
   .thehoya.com/for-30m-a-local-mansion-the-catch-may-come
   -with-ghosts-1.1893469#.UBgObO2hDHg.

## *West Point*

"Thayer Home." *HauntedHouses.com*. http://www.hauntedhouses.com
   /states/ny/thayer_home.htm
http://www.buzzle.com/articles/exploring-new-york-from-a
   -different-side-part-1.html
Brittle, Gerald Daniel. *The Demonologist: The Extraordinary Career of
   Ed and Lorraine Warren*. Lincoln, NE: iUniverse, 2002.

## *U.S. Naval Academy*

"Lieut. Sutton Suicide." *New York Times*, October 14, 1907. http://
   query.nytimes.com/gst/abstract.html?res=F00B14F9345417738D
   DDAD0994D8415B878CF1D3.
Hauch, Dennis William. *Haunted Places: The National Directory*. New
   York: Penguin Books, 2002.
Carter, Mike. "Ghost Stories: The Naval Academy." *The Capital
   Gazette*, October 16, 2007. http://www.capitalgazette.com/news
   /ghost-stories-the-naval-academy/article_a9b11151-79a8-51c1-
   bd0a-821508af4a3b.html.

### University of Ohio

Tremblay, Craig. *Guide to Ohio University Ghosts and Legends.* Lulu. com, 2007.

"Ohio University Haunted Halls." *The Post*, October 27, 2010. http:// thepost.ohiou.edu/content/ohio-university-haunted-halls

### University of Notre Dame

Nagy, John. "Haunt Thee, Notre Dame?" *Notre Dame Magazine*, Autumn 2009. http://magazine.nd.edu/news/12236-haunt-thee-notre-dame/

"The Ghost of Washington Hall." *University of Notre Dame.* http:// www.nd.edu/~washhall/ghost.html

"Haunted Indiana. Notre Dame University, South Bend, Indiana." http://www.prairieghosts.com/notre.html

Piarulli, Joe. "Gipp, Ghosts Haunt Campus Lore." *The Observer*, October 30, 2006. http://www.ndsmcobserver.com/2.2754/ gipp-ghosts-haunt-campus-lore-1.263820

# GET MORE AT LLEWELLYN.COM

Visit us online to browse hundreds of our books and decks, plus sign up to receive our e-newsletters and exclusive online offers.

- Free tarot readings • Spell-a-Day • Moon phases
- Recipes, spells, and tips • Blogs • Encyclopedia
- Author interviews, articles, and upcoming events

# GET SOCIAL WITH LLEWELLYN

**Find us on Facebook**

www.Facebook.com/LlewellynBooks

**Follow us on twitter™**

www.Twitter.com/Llewellynbooks

# GET BOOKS AT LLEWELLYN

## LLEWELLYN ORDERING INFORMATION

**Order online:** Visit our website at www.llewellyn.com to select your books and place an order on our secure server.

**Order by phone:**
- Call toll free within the U.S. at 1-877-NEW-WRLD (1-877-639-9753)
- Call toll free within Canada at 1-866-NEW-WRLD (1-866-639-9753)
- We accept VISA, MasterCard, and American Express

**Order by mail:**
Send the full price of your order (MN residents add 6.875% sales tax) in U.S. funds, plus postage and handling to: Llewellyn Worldwide, 2143 Wooddale Drive Woodbury, MN 55125-2989

**POSTAGE AND HANDLING:**
STANDARD: (U.S. & Canada)
(Please allow 12 business days)
$25.00 and under, add $4.00.
$25.01 and over, FREE SHIPPING.

INTERNATIONAL ORDERS (airmail only):
$16.00 for one book, plus $3.00 for each additional book.

Visit us online for more shipping options.
Prices subject to change.

**FREE CATALOG!**

To order, call
1-877-NEW-WRLD
ext. 8236
or visit our
website

# True Casefiles of a Paranormal Investigator
## STEPHEN LANCASTER

As a ghost hunter for nearly fifteen years, Stephen Lancaster's encounters with the paranormal range from the merely incredible to the downright terrifying. This gripping collection of true casefiles takes us behind the scenes of his most fascinating paranormal investigations. See what it's like to come face to face with an unearthly glowing woman in a dark cemetery, be attacked by invisible entities, talk to spirits using a flashlight, and dodge objects launched by a poltergeist. Every delicious detail is documented: the history and legends of each haunted location, what Stephen is thinking and feeling throughout each unimaginable encounter, and how he manages to capture ghost faces, spirit voices, a cowboy shadow man, otherworldly orbs, a music-loving spirit playing an antique piano, and other extraordinary paranormal evidence.

978-0-7387-3220-6, 240 pp., 5³⁄₁₆ x 8                    $15.95

VIVIAN CAMPBELL
STALKED by SPIRITS
true tales of a ghost magnet

# Stalked by Spirits
*True Tales of a Ghost Magnet*
VIVIAN CAMPBELL

Haunted since childhood, Vivian Campbell has encountered angry wraiths, mischievous child spirits, terrorizing demons, and all sorts of bizarre, unearthly beings. Vivian relives these chilling and thrilling experiences in *Stalked by Spirits*, including how she and her family suffered violent phantom attacks, received small favors from a little girl ghost, negotiated with a demanding spirit, welcomed back a dearly departed pet, tolerated ghostly attendance at holiday dinners and Girl Scout meetings, and waged hair-raising battles with an evil entity threatening their baby daughter.

Taking us inside a variety of spirit-infested, often beautiful places—a stone mansion in the Tennessee mountains, a century-old college dorm, the first apartment she shared with her new husband, and the beloved Florida home that's been in her family for generations—these true tales vividly capture an extraordinary and haunted life.

978-0-7387-2731-8, 288 pp., 5³⁄₁₆ x 8                     $15.95